THE ORACLE SPEAKS

THE ORACLE SPEAKS

Warren Buffett In His Own Words

EDITED BY DAVID ANDREWS

AN AGATE IMPRINT

CHICAGO

Copyright © 2012 by Agate Publishing, Inc.

No part of this book may be reproduced or transmitted in any form or by any means, electronic or mechanical, including photocopying, recording, or by any information storage and retrieval system, without express written permission from the publisher.

The Oracle Speaks is in no way authorized, prepared, approved, or endorsed by Warren Buffett and is not affiliated with or endorsed by any of his past or present organizations.

Printed in the United States.

Library of Congress Cataloging-in-Publication Data is on file with the Library of Congress.

10 9 8 7 6 5 4 3 2 1

B2 is an imprint of Agate Publishing. Agate books are available in bulk at discount prices. For more information, go to agatepublishing.com.

TABLE OF CONTENTS

Chapter 2: Wall Street and Speculation 43

INTRODUCTION

*When you get to my age, you'll really
measure success in life by how many of the
people you want to have love you actually
do love you. I know people who have a lot of
money, and they get testimonial dinners and
they get hospital wings named after them
and do all kinds of things. And the truth is
that nobody in the world loves them. If you
get to my age in life and nobody thinks well of
you, I don't care how big your bank account
is, it's a disaster.*

—WARREN BUFFETT

One could forgive Warren Buffett for lacking in modesty. From his office in Omaha, Nebraska—without even the benefit of a computer—he has racked up an investment record that far surpasses his counterparts on Wall Street, or anyone else in the world, for that matter. While the major stock indexes were gaining about 11 percent a year from the 1950s to the 1990s, Buffett was making investment choices that gained in value by about 29 percent a year, resulting in an investment business—Berkshire Hathaway—that is now the eighth-largest business in the world, and netting him $44 billion.

Yet the Oracle of Omaha speaks modestly of his own abilities. While he acknowledges that he has a unique ability to evaluate businesses, he doesn't feel entitled to the vast wealth that ability has earned him. Instead, he likes to say that he won the "ovarian lottery" by being born with the right skill set, to the right family, at the right place and time. Had he been born a few centuries earlier or somewhere in the developing world, his ability to allocate capital might have been worthless. That's one reason Buffett has pledged to give most of his money to charity, through the Bill and Melinda Gates Foundation as well as foundations run by his three children.

Even though Buffett speaks modestly of himself, he doesn't shy away from the limelight. He is more than willing to expound on his ideas about investment theory, current events, tax policy, or how to live a worthwhile life. He spends hours talking investments on CNBC, pens editorials in the *New York Times*, and shares colloquial stories in his annual report to Berkshire Hathaway shareholders (selections from each can be found on the following pages).

On investment, Buffett has a few rules. Look for businesses with an "enduring competitive advantage"—ones that could raise their prices tomorrow and not lose customers. Once you find one of those businesses, buy shares if the price is right, and then don't sell. One of the biggest mistakes investors make, he says, is frequently buying and selling stock and paying the broker fees that go with each transaction. That's one reason (besides a personal sense of loyalty) that Berkshire Hathaway almost never sells the stocks it buys, even when the businesses underperform.

Buffett's advice on life is simple, too. Find a profession you love, marry the right person, and love your family unconditionally. Believe in yourself, and don't listen too much to others. It's advice that Buffett has lived throughout his 80-plus years, bringing him not only a vast personal fortune, but more importantly, a loving and joyful life.

QUOTATIONS

CHAPTER 1: INVESTING

. . . .

Researching Investments

When I buy a stock, I think of it in terms of buying a whole company just as if I were buying a store down the street. If I were buying the store, I'd want to know all about it.

—Forbes, *November 1, 1969*

. . . .

Limiting Your Investments

In the investment world, if you had a punch card when you got out of school, and there were only 20 punches on it, and when that was done, you were all done investing, you'd make more money than having one with unlimited punches. You'd make sure you used them for the right things.

—*Lecture to Notre Dame undergraduate students,*
spring 1991

• •

Investment and Sports

I call investing the greatest business in the world, because you never have to swing. You stand at the plate, the pitcher throws you General Motors at 47! U.S. Steel at 39! And nobody calls a strike on you. There's no penalty except for the opportunity lost. All day you wait for the pitch you like; then when the fielders are asleep, you step up and hit it.

—Forbes, *November 1, 1974*

Ted Williams described in his book, *The Science of Hitting*, that the most important thing—for a hitter—is to wait for the right pitch. And that's exactly the philosophy I have about investing. Wait for the right pitch, and wait for the right deal. And it will come. It's the key to investing.

—*CBS News, February 8, 2012*

Degree of difficulty counts in the Olympics; it doesn't count in business. You don't get any extra points for the fact that something's very hard to do, so you might as well step over one-foot bars rather than try to jump over seven-foot bars.

—*CNBC, October 18, 2010*

• •

Thinking about Investment

The best way to think about investments is to be in a room with no one else and to just think. If that doesn't work, nothing else is going to work.

—*Colloquium at the University of Florida,*
October 15, 1998

• •

The Temperament of an Investor

Success in investing doesn't correlate with IQ once you're above the level of 25. Once you have ordinary intelligence, what you need is the temperament to control the urges that get other people into trouble in investing.

—BusinessWeek, *July 5, 1999*

• •

Studying Financial Data

If merely looking up past financial data would tell you what the future holds, the Forbes 400 would consist of librarians.

—*Letter to Berkshire Hathaway shareholders,*
February 2009

• •

Ordinary Competence, Extraordinary Results

What we do is not beyond anybody else's competence. I feel the same way about managing that I do about investing: It's just not necessary to do extraordinary things to get extraordinary results.

—Fortune, *April 11, 1988*

• •

The Simplicity of Investment

Draw a circle around the businesses you understand and then eliminate those that fail to qualify on the basis of value, good management, and limited exposure to hard times.

—Forbes, *November 1, 1974*

I don't know a thing now that I didn't know at 19 when I read [Benjamin Graham's *The Intelligent Investor*]. For eight years prior to that I was a chartist. I loved all that stuff. I had charts coming out my ears. Then, all of a sudden a fellow explains to me that you don't need all that, just buy something for less than it's worth.

—*Lecture to Notre Dame faculty, spring 1991*

I have this complicated procedure I go through every morning, which is to look in the mirror and decide what I'm going to do. And I feel at that point, everybody's had their say.

—The Snowball, *2008*

••

Beating the Market

There is no hunch or intuitiveness or anything of the sort. I mean, I try to sit down and figure out what the future economic prospects of a business are.

—*Colloquium with University of Nebraska–Lincoln students, October 10, 1994*

How do you beat Bobby Fischer? You play him at any game but chess. I try to stay in games where I have an edge.

—BusinessWeek, *July 5, 1999*

Most people can't do a couple percentage points better than the market. I'm telling people I still expect to do a little better than average, but nothing like I've done in the past. I wouldn't be running it if I thought I would be doing just average. That may be what happens, and I know that I can't do more than a couple points better than average. But it's better than most people do themselves. It may be better than I do.

—Haaretz, *March 23, 2011*

••

The Advantage of Having Less Money

If I was running $1 million today, or $10 million for that matter, I'd be fully invested. Anyone who says that size does not hurt investment performance is selling. The highest rates of return I've ever achieved were in the 1950s. I killed the Dow. You ought to see the numbers. But I was investing peanuts then. It's a huge structural advantage not to have a lot of money. I think I could make you 50 percent a year on $1 million. No, I know I could. I guarantee that.

—BusinessWeek, *July 5, 1999*

••

Idea Quota

My idea quota used to be like Niagara Falls—I'd
have many more than I could use. Now it's as
if someone had dammed up the water and was
letting it flow with an eyedropper.

—Forbes, *November 1, 1969*

When I got started, the bargains were flowing like
the Johnstown Flood; by 1969 it was like a leaky
toilet in Altoona.

—Forbes, *November 1, 1974*

∙∙∙

Long-Term Investment

I believe in owning productive assets ... whether it's farms, apartment houses, or businesses. And they'll do very well over time, and sometimes one class is doing better than another. But if you own any of those things over the next 20 years in the United States, I think you'll do well.

—CNBC, November 14, 2011

The future is never clear; you pay a very high price in the stock market for a cheery consensus. Uncertainty actually is the friend of the buyer of long-term values.

—Forbes, August 6, 1979

We don't want to own things where the world is going to change rapidly because I don't think I can see change that well or any better than the next fellow. So, I really want something that I think is going to be quite stable, that has very good economics going for it.

—Colloquium with University of Nebraska–Lincoln students, October 10, 1994

••

Speculation vs. Investment

There's nothing immoral or illegal or fattening about speculation, but it is an entirely different game to buy a lump of something and hope that somebody else pays you more for that lump two years from now than it is to buy something you expect to produce income for you over time. I bought a farm 30 years ago, not far from here. I've never had a quote on it since. What I do is I look at what it produces every year, and it produces a very satisfactory amount relative to what I paid for it. If they closed the stock market for 10 years and we owned Coca-Cola and Wells Fargo and some other businesses, it wouldn't bother me because I'm looking at what the business produces. If I buy a McDonald's stand, I don't get a quote on it every day. I look at how my business is every day. So those are the kind of assets I like to own, something that actually is going to deliver, and hopefully deliver to meet my expectations over time.

—*CNBC, March 2, 2011*

Reacting to Uncertainty

I do not think if Ben Bernanke comes up and whispers to me that he's going to do X, Y, or Z tomorrow, I'm not going to change my view about what businesses I want to own. I want—I'm going to own those businesses for years just like I would own a farm or an apartment house and there'll be all kinds of events and there'll be all kinds of uncertainties and in the end, what will really count is how that business or farm or apartment house does over the years.

—CNBC, November 14, 2011

Diversification

If your goal is not to manage money in such a way as to get a significantly better return than the world, then I believe in extreme diversification. So I believe 98 or 99 percent of people ... who invest should extensively diversify and not trade, so that leads them to an index fund type of decision with very low costs. All they're going to do is own a part of America and they have made a decision that owning part of America is worthwhile.

—Colloquium at the University of Florida,
October 15, 1998

If you really know businesses, you probably shouldn't own six of them. If you can identify six wonderful businesses, that is all of the diversification you need, and you're going to make a lot of money, and I will guarantee you that going into a seventh one . . . , rather than putting more money into your first one, has got to be a terrible mistake. Very few people have gotten rich on their seventh best idea.

—*Colloquium at the University of Florida,*
October 15, 1998

. . . .

Active Trading

Anything that causes people to think they can trade actively in stocks and do better than if they sat on their rear is a terrible mistake. American business has done wonderfully for investors over the years, yet many investors have managed to turn in bad performances. You can say to yourself, if the Dow started the 20th century at 66 and is now at 12,000, how could anybody lose money? But people do lose money. But they lose money by trying to jump in and out of this and that, and think that they should buy this stock because the earnings are going to surprise on the upside or some crazy thing like that. If they just buy good businesses, they'll do fine.

—*CNBC, November 14, 2011*

Wall Street makes its money on activity. You make your money on inactivity. If everybody in this room trades their portfolio around every day with every other person, you're all going to end up broke. The intermediary is going to end up with all the money. On the other hand, if you all own stock in a group of average businesses and just sit here for the next 50 years, you'll end up with a fair amount of money and your broker will be broke.

—Colloquium at the University of Florida,
October 15, 1998

If you own a farm and somebody said, you know, Italy's got problems. Do you sell your farm tomorrow? If you own a good business locally in Omaha and somebody says Italy's got problems tomorrow, do you sell your business? Do you sell your apartment house? No. But for some reason, people think if they own wonderful businesses indirectly through stocks, they've got to make a decision every five minutes.

—CNBC, November 14, 2011

As a class, [investors who use consultants and managers to trade stocks] must be *below* average. The reason is simple: (*a*) Investors, overall, will necessarily earn an average return, minus costs they incur; (*b*) Passive and index investors, through their very inactivity, will earn that average minus costs that are very low; (*c*) With that group earning average returns, so must the remaining group—the active investors. But this group will incur high transaction, management, and advisory costs. Therefore, the active investors will have their returns diminished by a far greater percentage than will their inactive brethren. That means that the passive group— the "know-nothings"—must win.

—*Letter to Berkshire Hathaway shareholders,*
February 2008

••

Investing and the Laws of Motion

Long ago, Sir Isaac Newton gave us three laws of motion, which were the work of genius. But Sir Isaac's talents didn't extend to investing: He lost a bundle in the South Sea Bubble, explaining later, "I can calculate the movement of the stars, but not the madness of men." If he had not been traumatized by this loss, Sir Isaac might well have gone on to discover the Fourth Law of Motion: *For investors as a whole, returns decrease as motion increases.*

—*Letter to Berkshire Hathaway shareholders,*
February 2006

• •

Buffett's First Stock

I bought my first stock when I was 11. I don't know why I waited so long, I was interested much earlier. But it took me until I was 11 to get the 120 bucks to buy it. I bought three shares of Cities Service, preferred at 38. It went to 27—you remember these things. My sister bought three shares with me. She couldn't stand the idea that I was going to get rich and she wasn't. We would walk to school and she kept reminding me as the stock went down. When it got back up to 40, I sold it. We each made $5 on our three shares. It went to 200 and something afterward. It doesn't pay to talk to your sister about your stocks on the way to school.

—Georgia Tech Alumni Magazine, *Winter 2003*

• •

Greed, Fear, and Buying

A simple rule dictates my buying: Be fearful when others are greedy, and be greedy when others are fearful.

—New York Times, *October 16, 2008*

••

When to Buy

I try to buy a dollar for 60 cents, and if I think
I can get that, then I don't worry too much
about when. A perfect example of this is British
Columbia Power. In 1962, when it was being
nationalized, everyone knew that the provincial
government was going to pay at least X dollars
and you could buy it for X minus, say, five. As it
turns out, the government paid a lot more.

—Forbes, *November 1, 1969*

Imagine if you owned a grocery store and you had
a manic-depressive partner who one day would
offer to sell you his share of the business for a
dollar. Then the next day because the sun was
shining for no reason at all wouldn't sell it for any
price. That's what the market is like and why you
can't buy and sell on its terms. You have to buy
and sell when you want to.

—Forbes, *November 1, 1969*

• •

Buying Today

Don't pass up something that's attractive today because you think you will find something way more attractive tomorrow.

—*Columbia University, November 12, 2009*

• •

Silly Market Behavior

The sillier the market's behavior, the greater the opportunity for the businesslike investor.

—*Preface,* The Intelligent Investor, *2003*

• •

Buying Troubled Companies

The best thing that happens to us is when a great company gets into temporary trouble. … We want to buy them when they're on the operating table.

—BusinessWeek, *July 5, 1999*

Buying in the Bad Times

On balance, we will do more business when people are pessimistic. Not because we like pessimism, but because it makes for prices that are much more attractive. If you all have filling stations to sell in South Bend, I want to do business with whomever is most negative about filling stations. And that's where I'm going to make the best buy. Times are really good and times are really bad, over a period of time. We don't quit selling candy in July just because it isn't Christmas.

—*Lecture to Notre Dame undergraduate students,*
spring 1991

Pricing Stocks

If you think something is worth a dollar, don't pay 99 cents for it. Buy it at 60 cents so there is a margin of safety. Don't drive up to a bridge that says capacity 10,000 pounds with a 9,900 pound truck and drive across it. Go down the road and find one that says 20,000 pounds.

—Georgia Tech Alumni Magazine, *Winter 2003*

Whether we're talking about socks or stocks, I like buying quality merchandise when it is marked down.

—*Letter to Berkshire Hathaway shareholders,*
February 2009

• •

The Most Important Question

We never buy something with a price target in mind. We never buy something at 30 saying if it goes to 40 we'll sell it, or 50 or 60 or 100. The way to look at a business is, is this going to keep producing more and more money over time? And if the answer to that is *yes*, you don't need to ask any more questions.

—*Colloquium at the University of Florida,*
October 15, 1998

●●●

A Bird in the Hand

Aesop was not much of a finance major, because he said something like, "A bird in the hand is worth two in the bush." But he doesn't say when. ... Sometimes a bird in the hand is better than two in the bush, and sometimes two in the bush are better than one in the hand.

—*The Snowball, 2008*

●●●

When Not to Buy

You shouldn't buy a stock, in my view, for any other reason than the fact that you think it's selling for less than it's worth, considering all the factors about the business.

—*Lecture to Notre Dame faculty, spring 1991*

• •

Buffett's Gas Station

Back when I had 10,000 bucks, I put 2,000 of it into a Sinclair service station, which I lost, so my opportunity cost on it's about 6 billion right now. A fairly big mistake—it makes me feel good when Berkshire goes down, because the cost of my Sinclair station goes down too.

—*Colloquium at the University of Florida,*
October 15, 1998

• •

When to Jump Ship

Should you find yourself in a chronically leaking boat, energy devoted to changing vessels is likely to be more productive than energy devoted to patching leaks.

—The Essays of Warren Buffett, *1997*

• •

Buffett's Birth and the Market

When I was born on August 30 of 1930, that was the high day for the whole year—242. It went straight down to 41. My mother must have felt guilty as hell witnessing what had happened.

—Charlie Rose, *September 30, 2011*

· ·

Hyperventilating at the Dow

It's amusing that commentators regularly hyperventilate at the prospect of the Dow crossing an even number of thousands, such as 14,000 or 15,000. If they keep reacting that way, a 5.3 percent annual gain for the century will mean they experience at least 1,986 seizures during the next 92 years.

—Letter to Berkshire Hathaway shareholders,
February 2008

· ·

The Market as a Voting Machine

In the short run [the market] is a voting machine; in the long run it's a weighing machine. Today on Wall Street, they say, "Yes, it's cheap, but it's not going to go up." That's silly. People have been successful investors because they've stuck with successful companies. Sooner or later the market mirrors the business.

—Forbes, November 1, 1974

• •

Splitting Stocks

If somebody really thinks that the stock is more valuable because we've split it, they're in the wrong show. It's like the guy who went into the pizza parlor and said, "I'd like a pizza." The guy says, "Shall I cut it into four pieces or eight?" And he says, "Better make it four, I couldn't eat eight."

—Georgia Tech Alumni Magazine, *Winter 2003*

• •

Uncertainty

The world's always uncertain. The world was uncertain on December 6th, 1941, we just didn't know it. The world was uncertain on October 18th, 1987, you know, we just didn't know it. The world was uncertain on September 10th, 2001, we just didn't know it. The world—there's always uncertainty. Now the question is, what do you do with your money? . . . If you leave it in your pocket, it'll become worth less—not worthless— worth less over time. That's certain.

—CNBC, *November 14, 2011*

••

Bonds

I do not like short-term bonds, and I do not like
long-term bonds. And if you push me, I'm sure
that I don't like intermediate-term bonds either.
I just think it's a terrible mistake to buy into
fixed-dollar investments at these kinds of rates.

—*CNBC, March 2, 2011*

••

Commodities

The problem with commodities is that you're
betting on what somebody else will pay for them
in six months. The commodity itself isn't going to
do anything for you.

—*CNBC, March 2, 2011*

· ·

Gold

Gold is a way of going along on fear, and it's been a pretty good way of going along on fear from time to time. But you really have to hope people become more afraid in [a] year or two years than they are now. And if they become more afraid you make money, if they become less afraid you lose money. But the gold itself doesn't produce anything.

—CNBC, March 2, 2011

You could take all the gold that's ever been mined, and it would fill a cube 67 feet in each direction. For what that's worth at current gold prices, you could buy all—not some—all of the farmland in the United States. Plus, you could buy 10 Exxon Mobils, plus have $1 trillion of walking-around money. Or you could have a big cube of metal. Which would you take? Which is going to produce more value?

—CNN, October 19, 2010

• •

The Value of Cash

On the back of the US dollar it says, "IN GOD WE TRUST." If Elizabeth Warren were in charge of the government printing office I think it would have to say, "IN GOVERNMENT WE TRUST," because that is all there is behind paper money. Governments can take actions that decrease the value of money and sometimes at a very, very rapid clip. And I think that's what many people are worried about in this country.

—CNBC, May 2, 2011

• •

Clinging to Cash

Those investors who cling now to cash are betting they can efficiently time their move away from it later. In waiting for the comfort of good news, they are ignoring Wayne Gretzky's advice: "I skate to where the puck is going to be, not to where it has been."

—New York Times, October 16, 2008

CHAPTER 2: WALL STREET AND SPECULATION

• •

The Value of Wall Street

The nature of Wall Street is that overall it makes a lot of money relative to the number of people involved, relative to the IQ of the people involved, and relative to the energy expended. They work hard, they're bright, but ... they don't work that much harder or [aren't] that much brighter than somebody that ... is building a dam someplace, you know, or a whole lot of other jobs.

—Remarks to the Financial Crisis Inquiry
Commission, May 26, 2010

. . . .

Investors in Wonderland

Many helpers [investment advisors] are apparently direct descendants of the queen in *Alice in Wonderland*, who said: "Why, sometimes I've believed as many as six impossible things before breakfast." Beware the glib helper who fills your head with fantasies while he fills his pockets with fees.

—*Letter to Berkshire Hathaway shareholders,*
February 2008

. . . .

Staying Sober in the Marketplace

You're dealing with a lot of silly people in the marketplace; it's like a great big casino and everyone else is boozing. If you can stick with Pepsi, you should be okay.

—Forbes, *November 1, 1974*

. . . .

Bad Ideas on Wall Street

Almost everybody I know in Wall Street has had as many good ideas as I have, they just had a lot of [bad] ideas too.

—*Lecture to Notre Dame faculty, spring 1991*

Bad Terminology

Bad terminology is the enemy of good thinking. When companies or investment professionals use terms such as *EBITDA* or *pro forma*, they want you to unthinkingly accept concepts that are dangerously flawed. (In golf, my score is frequently below par on a *pro forma* basis: I have firm plans to *restructure* my putting stroke and therefore only count the swings I take before reaching the green.)

—*Letter to Berkshire Hathaway shareholders,*
February 2002

The Lure of Speculation

It's always possible when you get a big asset class that moves on price that after a while, people forget about what the asset class represents and just get entranced with the fact that it went up a lot last week or last month and that their neighbor, who's dumber than they are, had made a lot of money and now their wife is telling them, you know, why aren't you in gold or whatever it may be that's—or Internet stocks.

—*CNBC, May 2, 2011*

. . . .

Profiting from Bubbles

We don't try to profit from bubbles. We just try
to avoid going broke from them, and so far we've
been OK.

—CNBC, May 2, 2011

. . . .

Peer Pressure and the Cause of Bubbles

When your neighbor has made a lot of money by
buying Internet stocks, you know, and your wife
says that you're smarter than he is and he's richer
than you are, you know, so why aren't you doing
it? When that gets to a point, when day trading
gets going, all of that sort of thing, very hard to
point to what does it.

—Remarks to the Financial Crisis Inquiry
Commission, May 26, 2010

•••

One More Bubble

You may recall a 2003 Silicon Valley bumper sticker that implored, "Please, God, Just One More Bubble." Unfortunately, this wish was promptly granted, as just about all Americans came to believe that house prices would forever rise.

—*Letter to Berkshire Hathaway shareholders,*
February 2008

•••

When Bubbles Burst

When times are good, it is kind of like Cinderella at the ball. She knew at midnight that everything was going to turn into pumpkins and mice, but it was just so much damn fun, dancing there, the guys looked better and the drinks got more frequent and there were no clocks on the wall. And that's what happened with capitalism. We have a lot of fun as the bubble blows up, and we all think we are going to get out five minutes before midnight, but there are no clocks on the wall.

—Haaretz, *March 23, 2011*

• •

Easy Money

When people think there's easy money available they're not inclined to change. Particularly if somebody said a month or two ago, "Watch out for this easy money," and then their neighbors made some more money in the ensuing month or two, it's just—it's overwhelming.

—Remarks to the Financial Crisis Inquiry
Commission, May 26, 2010

• •

Excessive Leverage

Excessive leverage leads to trouble. Wherever it pops up, not necessarily in the banking system—it can be in households—but the idea that you have to leverage yourself to buy something you can't pay for in its entirety, has its merits and limitations.

It's kind of like alcohol. One drink is fine, but 10 will get you in a lot of trouble. With leverage, people have a great propensity to use it because it's so much fun when it works. There should be some ways of controlling leverage, and that applies to individuals with home mortgages. The idea of people buying houses at 2–3 percent down is going to lead to trouble.

—Haaretz, March 23, 2011

• •

Addictive Leverage

When leverage works, it magnifies your gains. Your spouse thinks you're clever, and your neighbors get envious. But leverage is addictive. Once having profited from its wonders, very few people retreat to more conservative practices. And as we all learned in third grade—and some relearned in 2008—any series of positive numbers, however impressive the numbers may be, evaporates when multiplied by a single zero. History tells us that leverage all too often produces zeroes, even when it is employed by very smart people.

—Letter to Berkshire Hathaway shareholders,
February 2011

••

The Danger of Leverage

Extreme leverage has been, generally speaking, a net minus. The analogy has been made (and there's just enough truth to it to get you in trouble) that in buying some company with enormous amounts of debt, that it's somewhat like driving a car down the road and placing a dagger on the steering wheel pointed at your heart. If you do that, you will be a better driver—that I can assure you. You will drive with unusual care. You also, someday, will hit a small pothole, or a piece of ice, and you will end up gasping. You will have fewer accidents, but when they come along, they'll be fatal.

—*Lecture to Notre Dame undergraduate students,*
spring 1991

• •

Smart People and Leverage

If you don't have leverage, you don't get into trouble. That's the only way a smart person can go broke. I've always said if you're smart you don't need it and if you're dumb you shouldn't be using it.

—Remarks to the Financial Crisis Inquiry
Commission, May 26, 2010

• •

Derivatives

Long ago, Mark Twain said: "A man who tries to carry a cat home by its tail will learn a lesson that can be learned in no other way." If Twain were around now, he might try winding up a derivatives business. After a few days, he would opt for cats.

—Letter to Berkshire Hathaway shareholders,
February 2006

• •

Credit Default Swaps

They can be a very destructive instrument.
I mean, if you think about it, you can't go out and
insure my house against fire because you do not
have an insurable interest, as they call it in the
trade. Because once you insure my house against
fire and you may decide that dropping a few
matches around my lawn might be a good idea.
And credit default swaps, if you don't own under-
lying debt and you buy a credit default swap, you
have an interest in that place getting into trouble.

When a lot of people have an interest in a place
getting in trouble, they may start putting out mis-
leading statements about it. I mean, if you were
short the stock of a bank, and there wasn't any
FDIC, you might go out and hire 100 movie extras
to stand in front of that bank. And in effect, you
would create your own reality. Now buying credit
default swaps and talking about them and causing
the price of credit default swaps to go up creates
its own reality to some degree. So I think that they
are potentially a very antisocial instrument.

—*CNBC, November 14, 2011*

CHAPTER 3: BUSINESSES

· ·

Knowing Your Limits

If we have a strength, it is in recognizing when we are operating well within our circle of competence and when we are approaching the perimeter.

—Letter to Berkshire Hathaway shareholders,
March 2000

· ·

Pricing Power

The single most important decision in evaluating a business is pricing power. You've got the power to raise prices without losing the business to a competitor, and you've got a very good business. And if you have to have a prayer session before raising the price by a tenth of a cent, then you've got a terrible business.

—Remarks to the Financial Crisis Inquiry
Commission, May 26, 2010

••

Business Moats

A truly great business must have an enduring *moat* that protects excellent returns on invested capital. The dynamics of capitalism guarantee that competitors will repeatedly assault any business *castle* that is earning high returns. Therefore a formidable barrier such as a company's being the low-cost producer (GEICO, Costco) or possessing a powerful world-wide brand (Coca-Cola, Gillette, American Express) is essential for sustained success. Business history is filled with *Roman candles*, companies whose moats proved illusory and were soon crossed.

—*Letter to Berkshire Hathaway shareholders,*
February 2008

••

Understanding a Business

We don't do due diligence or go out kicking tires. It doesn't matter. What matters is understanding the competitive dynamics of a business. We can't be taken by a guy with a sales pitch. ... What really counts is the presence of a competitive advantage. You want a business with a big castle and a moat around it, and you want that moat to widen over time.

—BusinessWeek, *July 5, 1999*

My job is to look at the universe of things I can understand—I can understand Ike Friedman's jewelry store—and then I try to figure what that stream of cash, in and out, is going to be over a period of time, just like we did with See's Candies, and discounting that back at an appropriate rate, which would be the long-term government rate. [Then] I try to buy it at a price that is significantly below that. And that's about it. Theoretically, I'm doing that with all the businesses in the world—those that I can understand.

—*Lecture to Notre Dame MBA students,*

spring 1991

• •

Premium Businesses

One of the interesting things to do is walk through a supermarket sometime and think about who's got pricing power, and who's got a franchise, and who doesn't. If you go buy Oreo cookies, and I'm going to take home Oreo cookies or something that looks like Oreo cookies for the kids, or your spouse, or whomever, you'll buy the Oreo cookies. If the other is three cents a package cheaper, you'll still buy the Oreo cookies. You'll buy Jell-O instead of some other. You'll buy Kool-Aid instead of Wyler's powdered soft drink. But, if you go to buy milk, it doesn't make any difference whether it's Borden's, or Sealtest, or whatever. And you will not pay a premium to buy one milk over another. You will not pay a premium to buy one [brand of] frozen peas over another, probably. It's the difference between having a wonderful business and not a wonderful business. The milk business is not a good business.

—*Lecture to Notre Dame undergraduate students,*
spring 1991

The name *American Express* is one of the greatest franchises in the world. Even with terrible management it was bound to make money.

—Forbes, *November 1, 1969*

•••

Capital-Intensive Businesses

If you have a choice between going to work for a wonderful business that is not capital intensive, and one that is capital intensive, I suggest that you look at the one that is not capital intensive.

—*Lecture to Notre Dame MBA students, spring 1991*

•••

Finding Great Deals

The world isn't going to tell you about great deals. You have to find them yourself.

—*Columbia University, November 12, 2009*

•••

Newspapers

Let's face it—newspapers are a hell of a lot more interesting a business than, say, making couplers for rail cars. While I don't get involved in the editorial operations of the papers I own, I really enjoy being part of the institutions that help shape society.

—Wall Street Journal, *March 31, 1977*

• •

The Scuttlebutt Approach

I did a lot of work in the earlier years just in getting familiar with businesses. The way I would
do that is I would go out and use what Phil Fisher
called the *scuttlebutt approach*. I'd go out, I'd talk
to customers, I'd talk to ex-employees in some
cases, I'd talk to suppliers—everybody. Every time
I'd see somebody in an industry—let's say I was
interested in the coal industry. I'd go out and see
every coal company and I'd ask every CEO, "If you
were to only buy stock in one coal company that
wasn't your own, which would it be and why?"
And you piece those things together and you learn
a lot about the business after a while.

—*Colloquium at the University of Florida,*
October 15, 1998

• •

Don't Talk to Brokers

I read hundreds of annual reports every year.
I don't talk to any brokers—I don't want to talk
to brokers. People are not going to give you great
ideas.

—*Lecture to Notre Dame MBA students, spring 1991*

• •

Knowing What You Know

The important thing is to know what you know and know what you don't know. If you can extend the field of things that you know then so much the better. Obviously, if you understand a great number of businesses, then you have a better chance of succeeding than if you only understand a few.

The important thing is to know the perimeter of your circle of confidence and to play within that circle—the bigger the better. But if something isn't within my circle, I'm not going to be in that game. I found out about this Norwegian chess champion who's 20 years old. At 80 you would think that I'm better than him, but I'm not, and if I play him, he is going to beat me. He is going to beat me in about three moves.

There is no use letting your ego tell you that you are good at something that you are not. To the extent that I can draw that line accurately I'll do well, and to the extent that I won't, I won't. Take Apple, could I have seen what happened five years ago? No. Steve Jobs saw it. It was in his mind and other people's. I'll stick with what I understand.

—Haaretz, *March 23, 2011*

••

Growth vs. Profits

Charlie and I avoid businesses whose futures
we can't evaluate, no matter how exciting their
products may be. In the past, it required no brilliance for people to foresee the fabulous growth
that awaited such industries as autos (in 1910),
aircraft (in 1930), and television sets (in 1950).
But the future then also included competitive
dynamics that would decimate almost all of the
companies entering those industries. Even the
survivors tended to come away bleeding. Just
because Charlie and I can clearly see dramatic
growth ahead for an industry does not mean we
can judge what its profit margins and returns on
capital will be as a host of competitors battle for
supremacy. At Berkshire we will stick with businesses whose profit picture for decades to come
seems reasonably predictable.

—*Letter to Berkshire Hathaway shareholders,*
February 2010

• •

Buying Companies vs. Stocks

Charlie and I look for companies that have (*a*) a business we understand; (*b*) favorable long-term economics; (*c*) able and trustworthy management; and (*d*) a sensible price tag. We like to buy the whole business or, if management is our partner, at least 80 percent. When control-type purchases of quality aren't available, though, we are also happy to simply buy small portions of great businesses by way of stock-market purchases. It's better to have a part interest in the Hope Diamond than to own all of a rhinestone.

—*Letter to Berkshire Hathaway shareholders,*
February 2008

• •

Looking for "Elephants"

The universe I can't play in [i.e., small companies] has become more attractive than the universe I can play in [large companies]. I have to look for elephants. It may be that the elephants are not as attractive as the mosquitoes. But that is the universe I must live in.

—BusinessWeek, *July 5, 1999*

• •

See's Candy

Our See's candy is now $11 a pound thanks to my brilliance. ... Let's say there's candy available at $6 a pound. Do you really want to walk in on Valentine's Day and hand—I mean your wife has all these favorable images of See's candies over the years, ... and say, "Honey, this year I took the low bid," and then hand her a box of candy? It just isn't going to work.

—*Colloquium at the University of Florida,*
October 15, 1998

Coca-Cola and Happiness

Coca-Cola is associated with people being happy around the world ... : Disneyland or Disney World, at the World Cup, or at the Olympics—every place that people are happy. Happiness and Coke go together. Now you give me—I don't care how much money—and tell me that I'm going to do that with RC Cola around the world and have 5 billion people that have a favorable image about RC Cola? You can't get it done. You can fool around—you can do anything that you want to do—you can have price discounts on weekends and everything, but you're not going to touch it. And that's what you want to have in a business.

—*Colloquium at the University of Florida,*
October 15, 1998

· ·

The Taste of Colas

One thing that people don't understand is one thing that makes [colas] worth tens of tens of billions of dollars is one simple fact … : Cola has no taste memory. You can drink one of these at nine o' clock, eleven o' clock, three o' clock, five o' clock—the one at five o' clock will taste just as good to you as the one you drank earlier in the morning. You can't do that with cream soda, root beer, orange, grape—you name it. All of those things accumulate on you. Most foods and beverages accumulate on you. You get sick of them after a while. … And that means that you get people around the world that are heavy users, that will drink five a day or [with] Diet Coke maybe seven or eight a day or something of the sort. They'll never do that with other products, so you get this incredible per capita consumption.

—*Colloquium at the University of Florida,*
October 15, 1998

Hershey's

If you walk into a drugstore, and you say "I'd like a Hershey bar" and the man says "I don't have any Hershey bars, but I've got this unmarked chocolate bar, and it's a nickel cheaper than a Hershey bar," you just go across the street and buy a Hershey bar. *That* is a good business.

—*Lecture to Notre Dame faculty, spring 1991*

Gillette

Gillette is marvelous. Gillette supplies over 60 percent of the dollar value of razor blades in the world. When I go to bed at night and I think of all those billions of males sitting there with their hair growing on their faces while I sleep, that can put you to sleep very comfortably.

—*Colloquium with University of Nebraska–Lincoln students, October 10, 1994*

• •

The Daily Racing Form

The highest priced daily newspaper in the United States, with any circulation at all, is the *Daily Racing Form*. It sells about 150,000 copies a day, and it has for about 50 years, and it's either $2.00 or $2.25 (they keep raising prices) and it's essential. If you're heading to the racetrack and you've got a choice between ... Joe's Little Green Sheet, and the *Daily Racing Form*, if you're a serious racing handicapper, you want the *Form*. You can charge $2.00 for the *Form*, you can charge $1.50, you can charge $2.50, and people are going to buy it. It's like selling needles to addicts, basically. It's an essential business.

—Lecture to Notre Dame faculty, spring 1991

• •

The Walt Disney Company

Look at what Walt Disney was worth on the stock market in the first half of 1966. The price per share was $53, and this didn't look especially cheap, but on that basis you could buy the whole company for $80 million when *Snow White*, *Swiss Family Robinson*, and some other cartoons, which had been written off the books, were worth that much. And then you had Disneyland and Walt Disney, a genius, as a partner.

—Forbes, November 1, 1969

We bought 5 percent of the Walt Disney Company in 1966. It cost us four million dollars. Eighty million bucks was the valuation of the whole thing. ... *Mary Poppins* had just come out. *Mary Poppins* made about thirty million that year, and seven years later you're going to show it to kids the same age. It's like having an oil well where all the oil seeps back in.

Now the [numbers today are] probably different, but in 1966 they had 220 pictures of one sort or another. They wrote them all down to zero—there were no residual values placed on the value of any Disney picture up through the '60s. So [you got all of this] for eighty million bucks, and you got Walt Disney to work for you. It was incredible. But there it was.

And the reason was, in 1966 people said, "Well, *Mary Poppins* is terrific this year, but they're not going to have another *Mary Poppins* next year, so the earnings will be down." I don't care if the earnings are down like that. You know you've still got *Mary Poppins* to throw out in seven more years, assuming kids squawk a little. I mean there's no better system than to have something where, essentially, you get a new crop every seven years and you get to charge more each time.

—*Lecture to Notre Dame MBA students, spring 1991*

••

Making Money from the Internet

The Internet as a phenomenon is just huge. That much I understand. I just don't know how to make money at it. ... I don't try to profit from the Internet. But I do want to understand the damage it can do to an established business. Our approach is very much profiting from lack of change rather than from change. With Wrigley chewing gum, it's the lack of change that appeals to me. I don't think it is going to be hurt by the Internet. That's the kind of business I like.

—BusinessWeek, *July 5, 1999*

••

The Hype of Internet Companies

The Internet was going to change our lives, but it didn't mean that every company was worth $50 billion that could dream up a prospectus.

—Remarks to the Financial Crisis Inquiry
Commission, May 26, 2010

••

Textiles

Our textile business—that's a business that took me 22 years to figure out it wasn't very good. Well, in the textile business, we made over half of the men's suit linings in the United States. If you wore a men's suit, chances were that it had a Hathaway lining. And we made them during World War II, when customers couldn't get their linings from other people. Sears Roebuck voted us Supplier of the Year. They were wild about us. The thing was, they wouldn't give us another half a cent a yard because nobody had ever gone into a men's clothing store and asked for a pin striped suit with a Hathaway lining. You just don't see that.

—*Lecture to Notre Dame MBA students, spring 1991*

• •

Corporate Ethics

Three suggestions for investors: First, beware of companies displaying weak accounting. If a company still does not expense options, or if its pension assumptions are fanciful, watch out. When managements take the low road in aspects that are visible, it is likely they are following a similar path behind the scenes. There is seldom just one cockroach in the kitchen....

Second, unintelligible footnotes usually indicate untrustworthy management. If you can't understand a footnote or other managerial explanation, it's usually because the CEO doesn't want you to. Enron's descriptions of certain transactions *still* baffle me.

Finally, be suspicious of companies that trumpet earnings projections and growth expectations. Businesses seldom operate in a tranquil, no-surprise environment, and earnings simply don't advance smoothly (except, of course, in the offering books of investment bankers). Charlie and I not only don't know today what our businesses will earn *next year*—we don't even know what they will earn *next quarter*. We are suspicious of those CEOs who regularly claim they do know the future—and we become downright incredulous if they consistently reach their declared targets. Managers that always promise to "make the numbers" will at some point be tempted to *make up* the numbers.

—*Letter to Berkshire Hathaway shareholders,*

February 2003

• •

Exposed Companies

You only learn who has been swimming naked when the tide goes out.

—Letter to Berkshire Hathaway shareholders,
February 2008

• •

Risk and Human Nature

As long as human beings run institutions, including financial institutions, there will be people that take undue risks, there will sometimes be people that steal, there will be—you know, there will be people that don't understand the risks they're taking. It's just the nature of business.

—CNBC, November 14, 2011

• •

The High Road in Corporate America

Former Senator Alan Simpson famously said: "Those who travel the high road in Washington need not fear heavy traffic." If he had sought truly deserted streets, however, the Senator should have looked to Corporate America's accounting.

—Letter to Berkshire Hathaway shareholders,
February 2008

••

Inflated Earnings

For many years, I've had little confidence in the earnings numbers reported by most corporations. I'm not talking about Enron and WorldCom— examples of outright crookedness. Rather, I am referring to the legal, but improper, accounting methods used by chief executives to inflate reported earnings.

—New York Times, *July 24, 2002*

••

Dirty Corporate Laundry

It's the rinse cycle where you find out how dirty the laundry has been. We're in the rinse cycle of Corporate America, and we're finding out that there was more dirty laundry than we care to admit.

—Georgia Tech Alumni Magazine, *Winter 2003*

• •

Accounting for Stock Options

Whatever the merits of options may be, their accounting treatment is outrageous. Think for a moment of that $190 million we are going to spend for advertising at GEICO this year. Suppose that instead of paying cash for our ads, we paid the media in 10-year, at-the-market Berkshire options. Would anyone then care to argue that Berkshire had not borne a cost for advertising, or should not be charged this cost on its books?

—*Letter to Berkshire Hathaway shareholders,*
March 1999

• •

CEO Ethics

Most CEOs, it should be noted, are men and women you would be happy to have as trustees for your children's assets or as next-door neighbors. Too many of these people, however, have in recent years behaved badly at the office, fudging numbers and drawing obscene pay for mediocre business achievements. These otherwise decent people simply followed the career path of Mae West: "I was Snow White but I drifted."

—*Letter to Berkshire Hathaway shareholders,*
February 2003

CHAPTER 4: BERKSHIRE HATHAWAY

••

One Good Decision

If I can make one good decision a year, you know, we'll do OK.

—CBS News, February 8, 2012

••

The Importance of a Good Decision

When I make the decisions at Berkshire, I'm thinking about the fact that I've got 99 percent of my net worth in it and it's all going to charities so I mean, if I cause this place to go broke, there's a lot of downside to me.

—Remarks to the Financial Crisis Inquiry Commission, May 26, 2010

••

More Money than Ideas

Up until a few years ago, we sold things to buy more because I ran out of money. I had more ideas than money. Now I have more money than ideas.

—BusinessWeek, *July 5, 1999*

••

Making Mistakes

Mistakes don't bother me. I try to never do anything that would jeopardize the well-being of the whole place. So I build into the decisions I make the fact that I am going to make mistakes.

—Haaretz, *March 23, 2011*

I'll make more mistakes in the future—you can bet on that. A line from Bobby Bare's country song explains what too often happens with acquisitions: "I've never gone to bed with an ugly woman, but I've sure woke up with a few."

—*Letter to Berkshire Hathaway shareholders,*
February 2008

••

Never Looking Back

We never look back. You know, we just figure there's so much to look forward to, there's no sense thinking about what we might have—it just doesn't make any difference. I mean, you can only live life forward.

—*Colloquium at the University of Florida,*
October 15, 1998

••

Mistakes of Omission

I've made all kinds of huge mistakes of omission. The ones of commission show up in accounting. If I buy something for $1 and sell it for 50 cents, it shows up.... We've made relatively minor mistakes of commission. Those aren't the ones that bother me. The acts of omission that I'm talking about are things within my circle of confidence, things I could understand, did understand, and didn't do anything about. I was sucking my thumb. Those are the big mistakes.

—Georgia Tech Alumni Magazine, *Winter 2003*

••

Making Money Together

We want to make money only when our partners do and in exactly the same proportion. Moreover, when I do something dumb, I want you to be able to derive some solace from the fact that my financial suffering is proportional to yours.

—The Essays of Warren Buffett, *1997*

••

Structuring Deals

If I were to buy a farm and have someone run it for me, the deal I would make with the farmer in terms of what percentage of the crop he would get would be important. If I had someone managing an apartment building for me, my arrangement with him is important. It's important not only in terms of how the profits will be shared, it's important in assessing the person's attitude. You want someone running a place that looks at you as a partner and not as an adversary, and at Berkshire Hathaway, we really look at our shareholders as partners.

—Haaretz, *March 23, 2011*

Overseeing Berkshire's Businesses

We will never allow Berkshire to become some monolith that is overrun with committees, budget presentations, and multiple layers of management. Instead, we plan to operate as a collection of separately-managed medium-sized and large businesses, most of whose decision-making occurs at the operating level.

—*Letter to Berkshire Hathaway shareholders,*
February 2010

Holding on to Businesses

I don't like to sell. We buy everything with the idea that we will hold them forever. ... That's the kind of shareholder I want with me in Berkshire. I've never had a target price or a target holding period on a stock. And I have enormous reluctance to sell our wholly owned businesses under almost any circumstances.

—BusinessWeek, *July 5, 1999*

••

Selling Subpar Businesses

Regardless of price, we have no interest at all in selling any good businesses that Berkshire owns. We are also very reluctant to sell subpar businesses as long as we expect them to generate at least some cash and as long as we feel good about their managers and labor relations. ... Gin rummy managerial behavior (discard your least promising business at each turn) is not our style. We would rather have our overall results penalized a bit than engage in that kind of behavior.

—The Essays of Warren Buffett, 1997

••

No Exit Strategy

Unlike [leveraged buyout] operators and private equity firms, we have no "exit" strategy—we buy to keep. That's one reason why Berkshire is usually the first—and sometimes the only—choice for sellers and their managers.

—Letter to Berkshire Hathaway shareholders,
February 2003

Berkshire's Congregation

If I had a church and I was the preacher, and half the congregation left every Sunday, I wouldn't say, "Oh, this is marvelous, because I have all this liquidity among all my members! There's terrific turnover!" I would rather get a church were all the seats were filled every Sunday by the same people. Well that's the same way we look at the businesses we buy. We want to buy something that we're really happy to own virtually forever.

—Colloquium at the University of Florida,
October 15, 1998

Paying Berkshire's Directors

At Berkshire, wanting our fees to be meaning-less to our directors, we pay them only a pittance. Additionally, not wanting to insulate our directors from any corporate disaster we might have, we don't provide them with officers' and directors' liability insurance (an unorthodoxy that, not so incidentally, has saved our shareholders many millions of dollars over the years). Basically, we want the behavior of our directors to be driven by the effect their decisions will have on their family's net worth, not by their compensation.

—Letter to Berkshire Hathaway shareholders,
February 2003

....

Institutional Failure and CEO Compensation

You will always have institutions too big to fail, and sometimes they will fail in the next 100 years. But you will have fewer failures if the person on top and the board of directors who select that person and who set the terms of his or her employment if they have a lot to lose.

—Remarks to the Financial Crisis Inquiry
Commission, May 26, 2010

....

Inflating CEOs

Nobody knows in business whether you're batting .320 or not so everybody says they're a .320 hitter. And the board of directors has to say, well, we've got a .320 hitter, because they couldn't be responsible for picking a guy that bats .250.

—Remarks to the Financial Crisis Inquiry
Commission, May 26, 2010

• •

The Qualities of a Good Director

The current cry is for "independent" directors. It is certainly true that it is desirable to have directors who think and speak independently— but they must also be business-savvy, interested, and shareholder-oriented. In my 1993 commentary, those are the three qualities I described as essential.

Over a span of 40 years, I have been on 19 public-company boards (excluding Berkshire's) and have interacted with perhaps 250 directors. Most of them were "independent" as defined by today's rules. But the great majority of these directors lacked at least one of the three qualities I value. As a result, their contribution to shareholder well-being was minimal at best and, too often, negative. These people, decent and intelligent though they were, simply did not know enough about business and/or care enough about shareholders to question foolish acquisitions or egregious compensation.

—Letter to Berkshire Hathaway shareholders,
February 2003

••

How Not to Choose Directors

Consultants and CEOs seeking board candidates will often say, "We're looking for a woman," or "a Hispanic," or "someone from abroad," or what have you. It sometimes sounds as if the mission is to stock Noah's ark. Over the years I've been queried many times about potential directors and have yet to hear *anyone* ask, "Does he think like an intelligent owner?"

—*Letter to Berkshire Hathaway shareholders,*
February 2007

••

Overpaying CEOs

It's difficult to overpay the *truly* extraordinary CEO of a giant enterprise. But this species is rare. Too often, executive compensation in the United States is ridiculously out of line with performance. That won't change, moreover, because the deck is stacked against investors when it comes to the CEO's pay.

The upshot is that a mediocre-or-worse CEO—aided by his handpicked VP of human relations and a consultant from the ever-accommodating firm of Ratchet, Ratchet, and Bingo—all too often receives gobs of money from an ill-designed compensation arrangement.

—*Letter to Berkshire Hathaway shareholders,*
February 2006

••

Paying for CEO Performance

I am the compensation committee for 70-some companies which Berkshire owns. It's not rocket science. And we pay a lot of money to some of our CEOs, but it's all performance. When they make a lot of money it's performance related. And we have different arrangements for different people. But we've never hired a compensation consultant, ever. And we never will. If I don't know enough to figure out the compensation for these people, you know, somebody else should be in my job.

—*Remarks to the Financial Crisis Inquiry*
Commission, May 26, 2010

Replacing CEOs

It's almost impossible ... in a boardroom populated by well-mannered people, to raise the question of whether the CEO should be replaced. It's equally awkward to question a proposed acquisition that has been endorsed by the CEO, particularly when his inside staff and outside advisors are present and unanimously support his decision. (They wouldn't be in the room if they didn't.) Finally, when the compensation committee—armed, as always, with support from a high-paid consultant—reports on a megagrant of options to the CEO, it would be like belching at the dinner table for a director to suggest that the committee reconsider.

—*Letter to Berkshire Hathaway shareholders, February 2003*

CEOs and Negative Reinforcement

There should be more downside to the head of any institution that has to go to the federal government to be saved for reasons of the greater society. And so far, we have been better at carrots [than] sticks in rewarding CEOs at the top. But I think some more sticks are called for.

—*Columbia University, November 12, 2009*

CEO Perks

You've read loads about CEOs who have received astronomical compensation for mediocre results. Much less well-advertised is the fact that America's CEOs also generally live the good life. Many, it should be emphasized, are exceptionally able, and almost all work far more than 40 hours a week. But they are usually treated like royalty in the process. (And we're certainly going to keep it that way at Berkshire. Though Charlie still favors sackcloth and ashes, I prefer to be spoiled rotten. Berkshire owns the Pampered Chef; our wonderful office group has made me the Pampered Chief.)

—*Letter to Berkshire Hathaway shareholders,*
February 2007

Huge severance payments, lavish perks and out-sized payments for ho-hum performance often occur because comp committees have become slaves to comparative data. The drill is simple: Three or so directors—*not chosen by chance*—are bombarded for a few hours before a board meeting with pay statistics that perpetually ratchet upwards. Additionally, the committee is told about new perks that other managers are receiving. In this manner, outlandish goodies are showered upon CEOs simply because of a corporate version of the argument we all used when children: "But, Mom, all the other kids have one." When comp committees follow this "logic," yesterday's most egregious excess becomes today's baseline.

—*Letter to Berkshire Hathaway shareholders,*
February 2006

••

Managers Thinking Like Owners

I like guys who forget that they sold the business to me and run the show like proprietors. When I marry their daughter, she continues to live with her parents.

—Wall Street Journal, *March 31, 1977*

We have a business with very few rules. The only rules the managers have is to basically think like owners. We want those people thinking exactly like they own those businesses themselves. Psychologically, we don't even want them to think there is a Berkshire Hathaway.

—*Lecture to Notre Dame undergraduate students,*
spring 1991

• •

Berkshire's Managers

In 38 years, we've never had a single CEO of a subsidiary elect to leave Berkshire to work elsewhere. Counting Charlie, we now have six managers over 75, and I hope that in four years that number increases by at least two (Bob Shaw and I are both 72). Our rationale: It's hard to teach a new dog old tricks.

—*Letter to Berkshire Hathaway shareholders,*
February 2003

Managing Winners

My managerial model is Eddie Bennett, who was a batboy. In 1919, at age 19, Eddie began his work with the Chicago White Sox, who that year went to the World Series. The next year, Eddie switched to the Brooklyn Dodgers, and they, too, won their league title. Our hero, however, smelled trouble.

Changing boroughs, he joined the Yankees in 1921, and they promptly won their first pennant in history. Now Eddie settled in, shrewdly seeing what was coming. In the next seven years, the Yankees won five American League titles. What does this have to do with management? It's simple—to be a winner, work with winners.

—Letter to Berkshire Hathaway shareholders,
February 2003

Using Smart People

I don't have to be smart about everything; I didn't deliver my wife's baby! So, I believe in using people who are smarter than I am.

—Forbes India, April 20, 2011

••

Cost-Consciousness

We cherish cost-consciousness at Berkshire. Our model is the widow who went to the local newspaper to place an obituary notice. Told there was a 25-cents-a-word charge, she requested "Fred Brown died." She was then informed there was a seven-word minimum. "Okay," the bereaved woman replied, "make it 'Fred Brown died, golf clubs for sale.'"

—Letter to Berkshire Hathaway shareholders,
February 2003

••

Cutting Costs

Whenever I read about some company undertaking a cost-cutting program, I know it's not a company that really knows what costs are all about. Spurts don't work in this area. The really good manager does not wake up in the morning and say, "This is the day I'm going to cut costs," any more than he wakes up and decides to practice breathing.

—Fortune, April 11, 1988

· ·

Managing Workers

We've read management treatises that specify exactly how many people should report to any one executive, but they make little sense to us. When you have able managers of high character running businesses about which they are passionate, you can have a dozen or more reporting to you and still have time for an afternoon nap. Conversely, if you have even one person reporting to you who is deceitful, inept or uninterested, you will find yourself with more than you can handle. Charlie and I could work with double the number of managers we now have, so long as they had the rare qualities of the present ones.

—The Essays of Warren Buffett, *1997*

• •

Letting Managers Manage

Usually the managers [we hire] came with the companies we bought, having demonstrated their talents throughout careers that spanned a wide variety of business circumstances. They were managerial stars long before they knew us, and our main contribution has been to not get in their way. This approach seems elementary: if my job were to manage a golf team—and if Jack Nicklaus or Arnold Palmer were willing to play for me—neither would get a lot of directives from me about how to swing.

—The Essays of Warren Buffett, *1997*

There are many giant company managers whom I greatly admire; Ken Chenault of American Express, Jeff Immelt of GE and Dick Kovacevich of Wells Fargo come quickly to mind. But I don't think I could do the management job they do. And I know I wouldn't enjoy many of the duties that come with their positions—meetings, speeches, foreign travel, the charity circuit, and governmental relations. For me, Ronald Reagan had it right: "It's probably true that hard work never killed anyone—but why take the chance?"

—*Letter to Berkshire Hathaway shareholders,*
February 2007

••

The Reputations of Managers

When a manager with a reputation for brilliance meets up with a business with a reputation for bad economics, it's the reputation of the business that remains intact.

—*CNBC, October 18, 2010*

••

Jay-Z, Business Man

[Jay-Z is] a real business man. I'm just pretending.

—New York Times, *October 18, 2011*

••

Hiring

We don't hire because we get a tax break or because someone in the government tells us to. We hire when there's more demand for what we are making or moving or selling. It's that simple.

—*CNN, October 19, 2010*

• •

Enjoying Work

I have created something that I enjoy. ... It's a little crazy, it seems to me, if you are building a business and creating a business, not to create something you are going to enjoy when you get through. It's like painting a painting. I mean, you ought to paint something you are going to enjoy looking at when you get through.

—*Colloquium with University of Nebraska–Lincoln students, October 10, 1994*

CHAPTER 5: US POLICIES AND POLITICS

••

Betting on the United States

It's always been a mistake to bet against America, since 1776. And, you know, we take our body blows from time to time, but this country always comes through. And when we get united, get out of the way. And we are. At moments like this you particularly see that. And of course, after 9/11 we saw it. But I've always had enormous faith in this country to do anything, whether it's in economics or whether it's in liberating people or whatever it may be.

—*CNBC, May 2, 2011*

••

Economic Recovery

I think the big factor in the continuation of the recovery will be the Steve Jobses of the world coming up with new products that nobody thought of before. And millions of Americans doing what people before them have done, trying to think of ways to do them more efficiently. ... Capitalism works, and I think we're seeing it work.

—CNBC, May 2, 2011

GEICO got in trouble in the mid '70s. American Express got in trouble in the mid '60s. Those are two of the greatest investments I've ever had, and you had to look out five or ten years out. That's what you have to do with the economy, incidentally. We have a wonderful economy in the United States over time, and it will come back, just like GEICO came back and American Express came back.

—Charlie Rose, September 30, 2011

• •

The United States since 1930

I was born in August of 1930. You know, if a genie had come to me and said, "Warren, in the next two years, the Dow is going to go from 180 down to 40, there's going to be 4,000 banks closed. You know, there's going to be a dust bowl in Nebraska where you live, and farm prices are going to go to hell, and in another 10 years we're going to have a surprise attack by an enemy that looks like it's going to win the war for a while, we're going to have nuclear bombs"—you know, I'm not sure I would have come out. ... But the truth was that America, in the 80 years since I've been born, the average person lives six times better than when I was born. It's unbelievable what this country delivers. And we haven't—we haven't lost the magic potion at all. If anything, we've got more opportunity now than we've ever had.

—CNBC, July 7, 2011

I'm 80 years old, and in the 80 years since then, the average standard of living for Americans has improved six for one in real terms. Six for one! You go back to the Middle Ages, you went centuries and you were lucky if you were looking at a 1 percent increase. When I came out of the womb in 1930, we faced a depression, we faced a world war that it looked like we were losing, but the system works. It unleashes human potential.

—Haaretz, *March 23, 2011*

• •

The United States Solves Problems

If you look back on the 19th century, we had seven great bank panics. If you look back at the 20th century, we had the Great Depression and world wars and flu epidemics. This country doesn't avoid problems. It just solves them.

—*Columbia University, November 12, 2009*

• •

Economic Forecasts

I don't read economic forecasts. I don't read the
funny papers.

—BusinessWeek, *July 5, 1999*

We have never either bought a business or not
bought a business because of any macro feeling of
any kind. We don't read predictions about interest rates or business or anything like that because
it doesn't make any difference. I mean let's say
in 1972 when we bought See's Candy—I think
maybe Nixon put on the price controls a little bit
later. Let's say we'd seen that, but so what? We'd
have missed the chance to buy something for $25
million that's earning $60 million pre-tax now.
We don't want to pass up the chance to do something intelligent because of some prediction about
something that we're no good on anyway.

—*Colloquium at the University of Florida,*
October 15, 1998

••

Global Trade

There will be an element in the United States or in other countries that resists the idea of more trade between countries. I am in exactly the opposite camp and believe that we will prosper as we do more and more business with each other. Various countries have various advantages and no country can do all things themselves. As world trade expands it will mean a better life for people around the world.

—Forbes India, *April 20, 2011*

••

Creating Jobs

I'm very suspicious when people say, you know, "This will create jobs," and "If I open a hamburger stand, it'll create jobs." There's a lot of rhetoric that gets a little loose. If you're really seriously hurting the environment [to create 20,000 jobs], you can have those 20,000 people start building me a tomb.

—CNBC, *November 14, 2011*

••

Inflation

Inflation, someone said many years ago, is an invisible tax that only one man in a million really understands. It is a tax on people that have had faith in their currency, the governments issued it. The best investment against inflation is to improve your own earning power, your own talent. Very few people maximize their talent. If you increase your talent, they can't tax it or they can't take it away from you.

—Forbes India, *April 20, 2011*

Every time I get worried about inflation I think about how 94 percent of that dollar bill from when I was born isn't worth anything, yet I seem to have done pretty well, so it can't destroy everything.

—Haaretz, *March 23, 2011*

••

The 2008 Financial Crisis

People were watching a movie and they thought the movie had a happy ending and all of a sudden the events on the screen started telling them something different. And different people in the audience picked it up maybe [at] different hours, different days, different weeks. But at some point the bubble popped.

—Remarks to the Financial Crisis Inquiry
Commission, May 26, 2010

The American people, including banks, Congress, the administration, Freddie Mac and Fannie Mae, the media—they all subscribed to the idea that residential housing could not collapse. … It was a collective delusion, that once adopted, spread through all kinds of institutions and instruments of finance so that the interdependence of these items, once the delusion became exposed, once it became apparent that the emperor had no clothes, swept through the economy with the impact and the speed of a tsunami. All kinds of things happened that you wouldn't have thought possible because of this huge interdependence in markets.

—Haaretz, March 23, 2011

When it really became apparent that, you know, that this was something like we'd never seen was in September 2008. That's when I said on CNBC, "This is an economic Pearl Harbor." ... I meant that I hadn't seen it three months earlier because I didn't see a Pearl Harbor three months earlier.

—*Remarks to the Financial Crisis Inquiry Commission, May 26, 2010*

• •

Government Intervention in the Financial Crisis

Whatever the downsides may be, strong and immediate action by government was essential last year if the financial system was to avoid a total breakdown. Had one occurred, the consequences for every area of our economy would have been cataclysmic. Like it or not, the inhabitants of Wall Street, Main Street, and the various Side Streets of America were all in the same boat.

—*Letter to Berkshire Hathaway shareholders, February 2009*

Only the government could have saved things. The whole world wanted to deleverage. And they were deleveraging under conditions of extreme haste and with guns to their head in some cases. And the only entity that could possibly leverage up at the same time that everybody else wanted to deleverage was the federal government.

—*Columbia University, November 12, 2009*

We should thank Bernanke and Paulson and President Bush and President Obama and Tim Geithner for doing a lot of things that helped us get out of what could've been a terrible, terrible mess. It was a mess. But we really were right at the abyss and we had—we had a government that did the right things. Maybe they did some wrong things earlier, maybe they didn't do it perfectly. But I give them great credit and this country's best days lie ahead, believe me.

—*CNBC, November 14, 2011*

• •

Bank of America and the Financial Crisis

If [Bank of America CEO] Ken Lewis hadn't have bought Merrill on Sunday, I think the system would have stopped, you know. He is the guy that turned out to have saved the system.

—Remarks to the Financial Crisis Inquiry
Commission, May 26, 2010

• •

Opportunities during the Financial Crisis

I don't like to sound, you know, like a mortician during an epidemic or anything, but last fall [of 2008] was really quite exciting for me. I don't wish it on anybody, but there were things being offered. There are opportunities for us to do things that didn't exist a year or two earlier.

—Columbia University, November 12, 2009

• •

The Importance of Credit

Credit is like oxygen. When either is abundant, its presence goes unnoticed. When either is missing, that's *all* that is noticed. Even a short absence of credit can bring a company to its knees.

—Letter to Berkshire Hathaway shareholders,
February 2011

• •

Fraud in the Financial System

There was fraud on the parts of the borrowers and there were frauds on part of the intermediaries in some cases. But you better not have a system that is dependent on the absence of fraud. It will be with us.

—Remarks to the Financial Crisis Inquiry
Commission, May 26, 2010

••

Lending after the Financial Crisis

We were in the bar drinking. I'm not sure that we want to go all the way back in, but we ought to get over the hangover.

—Charlie Rose, *September 30, 2011*

••

The US Budget and Trade Deficits

We will not be spending 25 percent of GDP and raising 15 percent of GDP 10 years from now. We'll get there somehow. But … everybody in the country is trying to figure out how to have somebody else pay for it. But some of them are better equipped to fight that fight than others and they're the people with money that care and that hire lobbyists.

—CNBC, *November 14, 2011*

••

The Simpson-Bowles Plan

I think what happened with Simpson-Bowles
was an absolute tragedy. I mean, here are two
extremely high-grade people, they have somewhat
different ideas about government. But they're
smart, they're decent, they've got good senses of
humor, too. They're good at working with people.
They work like the devil for 10 months or something like that. They compromise, they bring in
people as far apart as Durbin and Coburn to get
them to sign on, and then they're totally ignored.
I think that's a travesty.

—CNBC, November 14, 2011

••

Government Debt

The important thing on government debt is how much is owed externally. ... The national debt is largely held internally, but the game is changing as we run a trade deficit. So the trade deficit is a threat, essentially, to living as well as we live now. We are, essentially, selling off a little piece of the farm every day, as we run a trade deficit in order to finance our own consumption. We've got a very big rich farm, so we can sell a little piece of that farm for a long time without hardly noticing it. It's a lot like eating a little too much over time. You never see it in any one day. You don't all of a sudden get up, all of your buttons pop, and people say "God, you look fat!" It just doesn't happen. What happens is you just keep doing it so pleasantly until, after a while, you've got a helluva waistline. And that is, essentially, the situation in our trade deficit. We are giving the rest of the world claim checks on us. That has consequences over time.

—Lecture to Notre Dame undergraduate students,
spring 1991

••

Raising the Debt Ceiling

We raised the debt ceiling seven times during the Bush administration and now in this administration, they're using it as a hostage. You really don't have any business playing Russian roulette to get your way in some other matter. We should be more grown up than that.

—*CNBC, July 7, 2011*

••

Democracy in the United States

We are still a democracy, but we have moved in my lifetime toward a plutocracy. We do not have a plutocracy, I want to emphasize that, but the distribution of wealth and the influence of wealth have moved in that direction.

—Haaretz, *March 23, 2011*

••

The Death of Osama bin Laden

A mass murderer of almost incomprehensible dimensions has been eliminated, just as was the case with Hitler. But there are lots of people in the world that are going to have evil intent toward this country … as well as other people, and they're not going to go away. And they're going to continue to seek ways to hurt us, disrupt us, and I think our government has done really quite an amazing job.

—*CNBC, May 2, 2011*

••

September 11, 2001

I really thought we were going to get hit again. And the reason we haven't been hit again, you know, we won't know all the reasons. But somebody has done a lot of things right … over the years, both administrations, to keep that from happening. But the desire to do us harm exists in the hearts of too many people around the world, and they're looking for new ways to do it, and we need an ever-vigilant government, and I think we have one.

—*CNBC, May 2, 2011*

Why, you might ask, didn't I recognize the [risk of terrorist attacks] *before* September 11th? The answer, sadly, is that I did—but I didn't convert thought into action. I violated the Noah rule: Predicting rain doesn't count; building arks does.

—*Letter to Berkshire Hathaway shareholders,*
February 2002

••

China

China and the United States, over time, will largely get along. We largely have the same interests. We both have nuclear bombs, so it's not in our interest to start getting really furious with each other. And there will be tensions. We'll want to play the game our way, and they'll want to play the game their way, and we'll both have to give in some cases.

—*CNBC, November 14, 2011*

• •

The Euro Crisis

They have tried an experiment where the imperfections in it are becoming manifest. ...
They melded into a single currency for 17 countries, but they didn't meld the culture, they didn't meld the fiscal policies. They either have to come closer together in a major way, or they need to separate.

—Charlie Rose, *September 30, 2011*

• •

Barack Obama

Looking back, he probably should have prepared the American public somewhat better for what laid ahead. ... There was not going to be some magic wand when he came in 2009. I admire him enormously and the actions taken, but to the extent that people thought we were going to cure everything in six months or eight months or ten months, that was a mistake.

—Charlie Rose, *September 30, 2011*

CHAPTER 6: WEALTH AND TAXES

••

Possessions

I have every possession I want. I have a lot of friends who have a lot more possessions. But in some cases, I feel the possession possess them, rather than the other way around.

—*CBS News, February 8, 2012*

••

Money's Magnifying Power

What money does is magnify you. Whatever kind of person you are going in—and age does this too as people get older—it magnifies both ... good and bad tendencies. Money gives you a chance if you're a slob to be a big slob—a huge slob. On the other hand, if you're inclined toward doing good things, it gives you the power to do a great many great things.

—Georgia Tech Alumni Magazine, *Winter 2003*

∙∙

Wealth and Satisfaction

As people get wealthy here, they start casting their eyes about, and they don't get more satisfied. Sometimes they get more dissatisfied. That's happened in the United States. Right now we have six times the GDP per capita, in real terms, as when I was born. Now, I don't know whether people are happier now or more discontent or what than they were in 1930. But people have a way of adjusting very quickly to things becoming better, and then any little tiny adjustment downward they can get quite unhappy about.

—*CNBC, November 14, 2011*

∙∙

Dividing the Economic Pie

Even in a rich family they may argue about who gets most of the income, and I am sure they do. We have a very rich family in the United States. The old would want more, the young would want more, the people who are in their productive years would like to give less to those who aren't. The pie will never be big enough to take care of everyone's desires.

—*Haaretz, March 23, 2011*

....

The Rising Tide of Wealth

We were promised that a rising tide would lift all boats. A rising tide has lifted all yachts.

—*CBS News, February 8, 2012*

....

The Source of Buffett's Wealth

My wealth has come from a combination of living in America, some lucky genes, and compound interest.

—*The Giving Pledge*

When we got married in 1952, I told Susie I was going to be rich. That wasn't going to be because of any special virtues of mine or even because of hard work, but simply because I was born with the right skills in the right place at the right time.

—Fortune, *June 25, 2006*

....

Inheritance

A very rich person should leave his kids enough to do anything but not enough to do nothing.

—Fortune, *June 25, 2006*

Neither Susie nor I ever thought we should pass huge amounts of money along to our children. Our kids are great. But I would argue that when your kids have all the advantages anyway, in terms of how they grow up and the opportunities they have for education, including what they learn at home—I would say it's neither right nor rational to be flooding them with money.

In effect, they've had a gigantic head start in a society that aspires to be a meritocracy. Dynastic megawealth would further tilt the playing field that we ought to be trying instead to level.

—Fortune, *June 25, 2006*

Wealth is just a bunch of claim checks on the activities of others in the future. You can use that wealth in any way you want to. You can cash it in or give it away. But the idea of passing wealth from generation to generation so that hundreds of your descendants can command the resources of other people simply because they came from the right womb flies in the face of a meritocratic society.

—The Snowball, *2008*

••

Buffett's Good Fortune

If all of us were stranded on a desert island—we all landed there and we were never going to be able to get off of it—the most valuable person would be the one who could raise the most rice over time. And I could say, "Well, I can allocate capital"—you wouldn't get very excited about that.

—Colloquium at the University of Florida,
October 15, 1998

I was born at the right time and place, where the ability to allocate capital really counts. I'm adapted to this society. I won the ovarian lottery. I got the ball that said, "Capital Allocator—United States."

—BusinessWeek, July 5, 1999

I have been lucky to have been born where I was … lucky with parents, lucky with all kinds of things, and lucky to be wired in a way that a market economy pays off like crazy for someone like me. It doesn't pay off for someone who is absolutely as good a citizen as I am—you know, leading Boy Scout troops, teaching Sunday school … raising fine families—but just doesn't happen to be wired in the same way I am.

—Colloquium at the University of Florida,
October 15, 1998

Wealthy People's Tax Rates

I'll bet a million dollars against any member of the Forbes 400 who challenges me that the average [tax rate] for the Forbes 400 will be less than the average of their receptionists. I'll give 'em an 800 number. They can call me. And the million will go to whichever charity the winner designates.

—NBC Nightly News, *October 30, 2007*

Forty percent of the revenue in the United States comes from payroll taxes, forty percent. My cleaning lady is being charged a payroll tax. Her payroll tax, counting the portion her employer pays, is higher than my capital gains tax. ... I mean, I am treated like I am the bald eagle or something— that I have to be protected at all costs.

—*CNBC, July 7, 2011*

Taxes for Hedge Fund Operators

[Hedge fund operators] say they work hard, and in the process of working hard, they make other people money. And that's true of a whole bunch of people in the world, but that doesn't entitle them to a preferential tax rate.

—NBC Nightly News, *October 30, 2007*

• •

Shared Sacrifice

Our leaders have asked for "shared sacrifice." But when they did the asking, they spared me. I checked with my megarich friends to learn what pain they were expecting. They, too, were left untouched. While the poor and middle class fight for us in Afghanistan, and while most Americans struggle to make ends meet, we megarich continue to get our extraordinary tax breaks.

—New York Times, *August 14, 2011*

• •

The Estate Tax

If you eliminate the $20 billion or so raised by the estate tax, you've got to make the money up by taxing everybody else somehow. It's amazing how the American population will fight for the families of those few thousand people who pay large estate taxes and for the whole rest of the country to pay for it out of their pockets.

—The Snowball, *2008*

• •

Berkshire's Tax Bill

Writing checks to the IRS that include strings of zeros does not bother Charlie or me. Berkshire as a corporation, and we as individuals, have prospered in America as we would have in no other country. Indeed, if we lived in some other part of the world and completely escaped taxes, I'm sure we would be worse off financially (and in many other ways as well). Overall, we feel extraordinarily lucky to have been dealt a hand in life that enables us to write large checks to the government rather than one requiring the government to regularly write checks to us—say, because we are disabled or unemployed.

—Letter to Berkshire Hathaway shareholders,
March 1999

• •

Revenue-Neutral Tax Reform

You can take the rate down and make it revenue neutral by knocking out all those special things. I have nothing against that. That would benefit Berkshire, frankly, but I will tell you, if it's going to be revenue neutral, it means just as many people are going to have their taxes increased as decreased, and the ones that are going to have them increased are going to be flooding the Capitol with lobbyists. If it's going to be revenue neutral, that means billions and billions and billions more are going to come from some companies, because we're going to pay less at Berkshire.

—*CNBC, November 14, 2011*

• •

Lobbying and the Tax Code

Every line in the tax code is there because someone was fighting for it. The people who care about that line are concentrated and focused on it, and people who are affected by that line are diffused and really not even aware of it.

—Haaretz, *March 23, 2011*

The tax law has been shaped not by logic, but by K Street.

—*CNBC, July 7, 2011*

. . . .

Income Inequality

If you look at these 400 top incomes that have gone from $40 million on average per family up to $200 million, their tax rate has gone from 29 and a fraction down to 21 percent. So there's been class warfare going on, it's just that my class is winning. In fact my class isn't just winning, we're killing them. It's been a rout!

—Charlie Rose, *September 30, 2011*

If there's a class war, you know, we're the ones that are waging it, the rich. And our soldiers are the lobbyists. And the poor have a bunch of little toy soldiers.

—*CNBC, November 14, 2011*

This system works for the people involved. It works for the wealthy, it works for the special interests, it works for people in Congress and it works for the lobbyists. And it may not work for my cleaning lady, but, you know, what can she do about it?

—*CNBC, November 14, 2011*

●●●

The "Buffett Rule"

In the last 25 years, the Forbes 400 list has had its net worth increase nine for one, nine for one. In the last 15 years, it's increased over three for one. That is not happening with the American people generally, and it's happening during a time when those same rich people have had their tax rates go down, down, down. And I think that when we're talking to 312 million Americans about shared sacrifice and taking away things we promised to them … it's time for the ultrarich to share in that sacrifice to some degree. They won't even feel it.

I mean, you change the Social Security rule somewhat and millions of people will feel it, they'll really feel it. You change the Medicare rules and millions of people will feel it. You get a minimum tax of 30 or 35 percent on incomes of a million or 10 million or over, the truth is, those people won't even feel it. But at least the American people, as a whole, will feel somehow that the ultrarich have been asked to participate to a small degree in this overall sacrifice that we're all going to be asked to participate in.

—*CNBC, November 14, 2011*

It's very important in terms of getting people to make the kind of sacrifices they're going to face. We're going to be telling people that some of the promises are going to have to be modified, and these are people that don't have a lot of margin of safety in their own affairs. They're not like me, they can't just sell a few stocks or something like that if the payment doesn't come through or this or that.

The ultrarich who are paying really subnormal taxes—and there's a lot of them that aren't, but there are a lot of them that are—I think it's a terrible mistake to ask 300 million Americans to tighten their belts and ignore that group.

—Charlie Rose, *September 30, 2011*

I'd rather have some home run that was hit in Yankee Stadium named after me. You know, "That was the Buffett Home Run" or something of the sort.

—*CNBC, November 14, 2011*

CHAPTER 7: LIFE LESSONS

• •

Unconditional Love

The biggest lesson I got is the power of unconditional love. If you offer that to your child you're 90 percent of the way home. If every parent out there can extend that to their child at a very young age—it's going to make for a better human being.

—The Huffington Post, *July 8, 2010*

• •

Buffett's Father

My dad ... he was really a maverick. But he wasn't a maverick for the sake of being a maverick. He just didn't care what other people thought. My dad taught me how life should be lived.

—The Snowball, *2008*

I never saw my dad do anything in his entire life that [he] wouldn't feel good about being on the front page of the paper. ... He gave me unconditional love. ... He was a terrific human being.

—*CBS News, February 8, 2012*

···

Buffett's Advantages

When I was a kid, I got all kinds of good things. I had the advantage of a home where people talked about interesting things, and I had intelligent parents and I went to decent schools. I don't think I could have been raised with a better pair of parents. That was enormously important. I didn't get money from my parents, and I really didn't want it. But I was born at the right time and place.

—The Snowball, *2008*

Childhood Rebellion

I was really rebelling [as a child]. Some of the teachers predicted that I was going to be a disastrous failure. I set the record for checks on deficiencies in deportment and all that. But my dad never gave up on me. And my mother didn't either, actually. Neither one. It's great to have parents that believe in you.

—The Snowball, 2008

Learning Ethics

I think the best place to learn ethics is in the home. I think most of us get our values from what we see around us before we get to business school. I think that it's important to emphasize them, but I think that if I had a choice of having great education and ethics fully on in the home or as a course in a school later on, I would choose the home.

—Columbia University, November 12, 2009

Buffett's Wife

Susie was as big an influence on me as my dad, or bigger probably, in a different way. I had all these defense mechanisms that she could explain, but I can't. She probably saw things in me that other people couldn't see. But she knew it would take time and a lot of nourishment to bring it out. She made me feel that I had somebody with a little sprinkling can who was going to make sure that the flowers grew.

—*The Snowball, 2008*

Whom to Marry

Marry the right person. And I'm serious about that. It will make more difference in your life. It will change your aspiration, all kind of things. It's enormously important who you marry.

—*Columbia University, November 12, 2009*

Life Plans

I don't believe in making life plans.

—Forbes, *November 1, 1969*

Teasing Jay-Z

Jay-Z had been out here about a year ago. And what I did was I admired his tie about six times. I said, "Boy, that is a good-looking tie, Jay." And finally he said, "OK, you win, Warren." And he took it off and he gave it to me.

[Later] I went to this opening. I wore the tie he gave me. And then, when I saw him, I started looking at his tie. And I said, "You know, Jay, that is one good-looking tie." And he said, "Warren ... forget it, you only get one."

—*CBS News, February 8, 2012*

Daily Routine

I spend an inordinate amount of time reading. I probably read at least six hours a day, maybe more. And I spend an hour or two on the telephone. And I think. That's about it.

—*Colloquium with University of Nebraska–Lincoln students, October 10, 1994*

Patience

[Capital Cities/ABC CEO] Tom Murphy, 40 years ago, said to me one day, "You know, Warren, you can tell a guy to go to hell tomorrow. You don't give up the right. So just keep your mouth shut today, and see if you feel the same way tomorrow." That's terrific advice. I don't know how many problems that's saved me.

—The Huffington Post, *July 8, 2010*

Belief in Oneself

I feel like I'm on my back and there's the Sistine Chapel, and I'm painting away. I like it when people say, "Gee, that's a pretty good-looking painting." But it's my painting, and when somebody says, "Why don't you use more red instead of blue?" Goodbye. It's my painting. And I don't care what they sell it for. The painting itself will never be finished. That's one of the great things about it.

—The Snowball, *2008*

I do not believe in taking baby steps when you see something that you really understand. I never want to do anything on a small scale because, what's the reason? If I'm doing it on a small scale because I'm not that sure of my opinion, I'll forget it entirely and go on to something I'm sure about.

—*Colloquium with University of Nebraska–Lincoln students, October 10, 1994.*

• •

Whom Buffett Listens To

I was lucky enough to get the right foundation very early on. And then basically I didn't listen to anybody else. I just look in the mirror every morning and the mirror always agrees with me.

—*Columbia University, November 12, 2009*

· ·

The Inner Scorecard

The big question about how people behave is whether they've got an Inner Scorecard or an Outer Scorecard. It helps if you can be satisfied with an Inner Scorecard. I always pose it this way. I say: "Lookit. Would you rather be the world's greatest lover, but have everyone think you're the world's worst lover? Or would you rather be the world's worst lover but have everyone think you're the world's greatest lover?"

—The Snowball, *2008*

· ·

Your Best Investment

Your best investment is yourself. There is nothing that compares to it.

—Georgia Tech Alumni Magazine, *Winter 2003*

· ·

Unpleasant Work

If you work with people who cause your stomach to churn, I'd say get another job. That is a terrible way to go through life, and you only go through life once.

—Georgia Tech Alumni Magazine, *Winter 2003*

• •

Loving Your Work

You gotta do what you love. You've got to have a passion for it. If you're not doing it, get into something else. There is something out there for you. ... As long as you are doing something that you enjoy, it doesn't really make a difference whether you've got $10 million or $100 million or $1 million. You want to have enough so you can do most of the things in life you like doing. That doesn't take a fortune.

—Georgia Tech Alumni Magazine, *Winter 2003*

Do what you would do if you were in my position, where the money means nothing to you. At 79 ... I work every day. And it's what I want to do more than anything else in the world. The closer you can come to that early on in your life, you know the more fun you're going to have in life and really the better you're going to do.

—*Columbia University, November 12, 2009*

••

Integrity

There was a fellow that—Pete Kiewit, in Omaha—
used to say that he looked for three things in
hiring people. He looked for integrity, intelligence,
and energy. And he said if a person didn't have the
first ... that the latter two would kill him. Because
if they don't have integrity, you want 'em dumb
and lazy. You don't want 'em smart and energetic.

—Colloquium at the University of Florida,
October 15, 1998

• •

Qualities for Success

Think for a moment that I granted you the right to buy 10 percent of one of your classmates for the rest of his or her lifetime … and I gave you an hour to think about it. Which one are you going to pick …? Are you going to give them an IQ test? Pick the one with the highest IQ? I doubt it. Are you going to pick the one with the best grades? I doubt it. You're not even going to pick the most energetic one necessarily or the one that displays initiative, but you're going to start looking for qualitative factors in addition, because everyone has enough brain power and energy. … You'd probably pick the one who you responded the best to. The one that was going to have the leadership qualities. The one that was going to be able to get other people to carry out their interests. That would be the person who was generous and honest, and who gave credit to other people even for their own ideas. All kinds of qualities like that.

—Colloquium at the University of Florida,
October 15, 1998

••

Temperament

By far, the most important quality is not how much IQ you've got. IQ is not the scarce factor. You need a reasonable amount of intelligence, but the *temperament* is 90 percent of it.

—Lecture to Notre Dame faculty, spring 1991

••

Old Age

When you're 81, you're gonna have more fun than you're having now. I mean, 81 is a great year. I look forward to doing what I do. ... I forget whether it was Mel Ott, when he was playing for the Giants or somebody, said, "You know, they—you mean they pay me for this?" That's the way I feel.

—CBS News, February 8, 2012

••

Measuring Success

When you get to my age, you'll really measure success in life by how many of the people you want to have love you actually do love you. I know people who have a lot of money, and they get testimonial dinners and they get hospital wings named after them. But the truth is that nobody in the world loves them. If you get to my age in life and nobody thinks well of you, I don't care how big your bank account is, [your life] is a disaster.

—Georgia Tech Alumni Magazine, *Winter 2003*

• •

Taking Care of Yourself

Let's say that when I turned 16, a genie appeared to me. And that genie says, "Warren, I'm going to give you the car of your choice. It'll be here tomorrow morning with a big bow tied on it. Brand-new. And it's all yours." Having heard all these genie stories, I would say, "What's the catch?" And the genie would answer, "There's only one catch. This is the last car you're ever going to get in your life. So it's got to last a lifetime."

If that happened, I would have picked out that car. But, can you imagine, knowing it had to last a lifetime, what I would do with it? I would read the manual about five times. I would always keep it garaged. If there was the least little dent or scratch, I'd have it fixed right away because I wouldn't want it rusting. I would baby that car, because it would have to last a lifetime.

That's the position you're in concerning your mind and body. You only get one mind and body. And it's got to last a lifetime. Now, it's very easy to let them ride for many years. But if you don't take care of that mind and that body, they'll be a wreck 40 years later, just like the car would be. It's what you do right now, today, that determines how your mind and body will operate 10, 20, and 30 years from now.

—The Snowball, 2008

The Forbes List

If *Forbes* would put a list of the 400 oldest Americans and I was on that one—that's the list I really want to be on.

—*CNBC, May 2, 2011*

Retiring

I'm in very good health, I love what I do and I'll go gaga someday and they'll yank me out of here. . . . My three kids are supposed to come in as a group and say, "You know, you're going gaga, Dad." I tell them if only one comes in, they're out of the will, so they have to come in as a group.

—*CNBC, November 14, 2011*

Managing Posthumously

I've reluctantly discarded the notion of my continuing to manage the portfolio after my death—abandoning my hope to give new meaning to the term "thinking outside the box."

—*Letter to Berkshire Hathaway shareholders,*
February 2008

••

The Challenges of Philanthropy

In business you are looking for easy problems. In philanthropy you are looking for very tough problems. If you are doing serious, big philanthropy, you are looking at problems that defied intellect for a long time and people have known they were important. So you've got to expect way more failure.

In my letter to my children, when I set up their philanthropic institutions, I said, if all your efforts are successful, then you are a failure, because it just means you are doing easy things that society would get done anyway.

But one big problem, aside from the fact that you're tackling way harder problems, the second problem is you do not have a market system feedback. You set up a hamburger stand and you are turning out lousy hamburgers, you will know it by the end of the day. In philanthropy, if you are doing something dumb, you will have people encouraging you to do more of the dumb thing. So, it has no market feedback, and that's a huge issue.

—Haaretz, *March 23, 2011*

• •

Giving Back to Society

Andrew Carnegie ... said that huge fortunes that flow in large part from society should in large part be returned to society. In my case, the ability to allocate capital would have had little utility unless I lived in a rich, populous country in which enormous quantities of marketable securities were traded and were sometimes ridiculously mispriced. And fortunately for me, that describes the United States in the second half of the last century.

—Fortune, *June 25, 2006*

• •

Giving to the Gates Foundation

I came to realize that there was a terrific foundation that was already scaled up—that wouldn't have to go through the real grind of getting to a megasize like the Buffett Foundation would—and that could productively use my money now. . . .

Over the years I had gotten to know Bill and Melinda Gates well, spent a lot of time with them having fun, and way beyond that, had grown to admire what they were doing with their foundation. I've seen them give presentations about its programs, and I'm always amazed at the enthusiasm and passion and energy they're pouring into their work. They've gone at it, you might say, with both head and heart.

—Fortune, *June 25, 2006*

He has this view that every human life worldwide is the equivalent of every other human life, and he's backing it up not only with money, but backing it up with his time. And his wife, Melinda, is backing it up with her time. And they are really going to spend, you know, the last half of their lives or so using ... money, talent, energy, imagination, all improving the lives of 6.5 billion people around the world. That's what I admire the most.

—Columbia University, November 12, 2009

I'm getting two people enormously successful at something, where I've had a chance to see what they've done, where I know they will keep doing it—where they've done it with their own money, so they're not living in some fantasy world—and where in general I agree with their reasoning. If I've found the right vehicle for my goal, there's no reason to wait.

Compare what I'm doing with them to my situation at Berkshire, where I have talented and proven people in charge of our businesses. They do a much better job than I could in running their operations. What can be more logical, in whatever you want done, than finding someone better equipped than you are to do it? Who wouldn't select Tiger Woods to take his place in a high-stakes golf game?

—Fortune, June 25, 2006

··

A Fair Society

Let's just assume that it was 24 hours before you were born and a genie came to you and he said, "Herb, you look very promising and I've got a big problem. I've got to design the world in which you're going to live and ... I've decided ... it's too tough, *you* design it." ... You figure out what the social rules should be, the economic rules, the governmental rules, and you're going to live under those, your kids are going to live under them, and their kids are going to live under them. You say, "I can design anything? ... There must be a catch." He says, "Well, there is a catch. You don't know whether you're going to be born black or white, rich or poor, male or female, infirm or able-bodied. ... All you know, is you're going to take one ball out of a barrel that's got 5.8 billion."

You're going to participate in what I call the *ovarian lottery*. You're going to get one ball out of there and that is the most important thing that's ever going to happen to you in your life. That is going to control whether you're born here or in Afghanistan, or whether you're born with an IQ of 130 or an IQ of 70. It's going to determine a whole lot. And you're going to go out into that world and you're going to have that ball. Now what kind of a world do you want to design?

I think that's a good way to look at social questions, because not knowing what ball you're going to get, you're going to want to design a system that includes lots of goods and services, because you're going to want people—on balance—to live well. And you're going to want it to produce more and more so your kids are going to live well and your grandchildren are going to live better than your kids, but you're also going to want a system that … does not leave behind a person who accidentally got the wrong ball.

—*Colloquium at the University of Florida,*
October 15, 1998

MILESTONES

August 30, 1930

Warren Edward Buffett is born in Nebraska to Howard and Leila Buffett.

1941

WB, 11, buys his first shares of stock with his sister, Doris. After the shares initially lose value, WB sells them at a modest profit. Shortly after he sells them, the price per share goes up by more than 500 percent.

1942

WB moves to Washington, DC, with his family when his father is elected to Congress.

1945

WB invests $1,200 of savings in 40 acres of farmland, using money earned from delivering newspapers.

1947

WB and a friend start a business enterprise. They purchase secondhand pinball machines, place them in local stores, including a barber shop, and collect the profits. WB sells the business.

After graduating from high school, WB enrolls at the Wharton School in Pennsylvania. He complains that he knows more than his teachers.

1949

WB transfers to the University of Nebraska–Lincoln, where he graduates after three years of college.

WB reads Benjamin Graham's *The Intelligent Investor*, which he credits with teaching him the investment philosophies he uses throughout his life.

1950

WB enrolls at Columbia University after learning that Graham is a professor there.

1951

WB offers to work for Graham for free but is turned down. He graduates and returns to Omaha, where he begins dating Susan Thompson. WB invests $2,000 in a Sinclair service station, where he washes windshields on weekends. He loses the entire investment.

1952

WB and Susan Thompson marry and have their first child, Susie.

1954

Graham offers WB a job in his partnership, which he joins for a salary of $12,000 per year. The family moves to White Plains, New York, and WB becomes the partnership's star performer.

1956

Graham retires and offers to make WB a partner in his business. WB, tired of New York and not interested in being a junior partner, turns him down.

The family returns to Omaha, and WB decides to retire and live off the interest of his money. To earn enough money to retire, WB creates Buffett Associates, an investment partnership, with several friends. He then creates two more partnerships.

1957

WB creates two more investment partnerships, bringing the total to five.

1961

WB makes his first investment worth more than $1 million.

1962

WB merges his partnerships into Buffett Partnerships, which is now worth around $7 million.
WB begins to buy stock in the textile manufacturing company Berkshire Hathaway.

1964

A fraud scandal brings the price of American Express stock down. WB begins buying shares, confident in the company and its long-term prospects.

1965

WB invests heavily in the Walt Disney company, believing strongly in the future profitability of the company and the leadership qualities of Walt Disney himself, whom WB meets.

WB takes control of Berkshire Hathaway and names a new president to run the company.

1969

WB dissolves his various partnerships and distributes shares of stock in Berkshire Hathaway to his partners.

1970

Berkshire Hathaway's earnings from insurance and various investments are more than one hundred times as great as its textiles earnings.
WB begins writing annual letters to Berkshire Hathaway shareholders.

1977

Berkshire Hathaway acquires the *Buffalo Evening News*—while already having an interest in other newspapers, such as the *Washington Post*. This gives rise to antitrust claims that never materialize.

1983

Berkshire Hathaway stock rises past $1,000 per share. WB's net worth reaches $620 million.

1985

WB shuts down Berkshire textile mills after years of propping up the failing business.

1988

Berkshire Hathaway begins buying over $1 billion of Coca-Cola stock.

1990

Berkshire Hathaway buys 10 percent of Wells Fargo.

1995

Berkshire Hathaway acquires Helzberg Diamonds and RC Willey Home Furnishings.

1996

Berkshire Hathaway fully acquires GEICO insurance company.

1997

Berkshire Hathaway acquires Dairy Queen and Star Furniture, and invests in US Airways.

1998

Berkshire Hathaway acquires General Re and Executive Jet.

1999

Berkshire Hathaway acquires Jordan's Furniture and invests in MidAmerican Energy Holdings Company.

2000

WB named the top money manager of the 20th century by the Carson Group.

Berkshire Hathaway acquires Acme Building Brands, Shaw Industries, Benjamin Moore, and Johns Manville.

2004

WB's wife, Susan, dies of a stroke.

2006

WB announces his plan to give more than 80 percent of his fortune to five foundations, the largest part going to the Bill and Melinda Gates Foundation.

WB marries Astrid Menks.

2006

WB auctions off his 2001 Lincoln Town Car for charity.

2007

WB announces that he is searching for a successor to run Berkshire Hathaway.

2008

WB becomes the richest man in the world.

With the stock market crashing, WB invests $5 billion in Goldman Sachs.

2010

WB, Bill Gates, and Facebook CEO Mark Zuckerberg sign the Giving Pledge, promising to give away at least half of their accumulated wealth over time.

2011

After WB argues that the taxes of wealthy Americans are too low, Barack Obama advocates the "Buffett Rule," a tax plan that would set a new tax rate for individuals earning more than $1 million per year.

2012

WB discloses that he has stage 1 prostate cancer and will undergo radiation treatment.

Berkshire Hathaway Public Holdings

April 4, 2012

Company	Holding Value	Stake
The Coca-Cola Company (KO)	$14.69 billion	8.8%
International Business Machines (IBM)	$13.17 billion	5.4%
Wells Fargo (WFC)	$12.99 billion	13.0%
American Express (AXP)	$8.69 billion	2.8%
Proctor & Gamble	$5.16 billion	2.8%
Kraft Foods	$3.32 billion	4.9%
Wal-Mart Stores	$2.36 billion	1.1%
ConocoPhillips	$2.22 billion	2.3%
U.S. Bancorp	$2.16 billion	2.3%
Johnson & Johnson	$1.90 billion	1.1%
Moody's Corp	$1.20 billion	12.8%
DIRECTV	$995 million	2.9%
Washington Post Co.	$645 million	22.4%
M&T Bank Corp	$465 million	4.3%
Costco Wholesale Corp	$386 million	1.0%
Visa Inc.	$341 million	0.35%
Intel Corp.	$321 million	0.23%
CVS Caremark	$315 million	0.55%
USG Corp	$283 million	16.2%
General Dynamics	$281 million	1.1%
DaVita Inc.	$233 million	2.9%
Dollar General	$210 million	1.3%

(*continued*)

Company	Holding Value	Stake
Torchmark	$208 million	4.2%
MasterCard Inc.	$174 million	0.3%
Verisk Analytics	$162 million	1.9%
General Electric	$153 million	0.07%
Sanofi SA	$153 million	0.15%
Liberty Media	$149 million	1.4%
United Parcel Service	$114 million	0.15%
GlaxoSmithKline	$68 million	0.06%
Bank of New York Mellon	$43 million	0.15%
Ingersoll Rand	$26 million	0.2%
Gannett	$26 million	0.73%

Source: CNBC, Warren Buffet Watch. www.cnbc.com/id/22130601/

Subsidiaries of Berkshire Hathaway

Insurance
    GEICO
    General Re
    Berkshire Hathaway Reinsurance Group
    Berkshire Hathaway Primary Group
Railroad
    Burlington Northern Santa Fe
Utilities and Energy
    MidAmerican Energy Holdings
Manufacturing
    Marmon (manufacturing and service businesses)
    McLane Company (grocery and product distribution)
    Acme Building Brands
    Benjamin Moore
    Johns Manville (building products)
    Shaw (building products)
    MiTek (building products)
    Fruit of the Loom
    Forest River (leisure vehicles)
    IMC Metalworking Companies
    Lubrizol (chemicals)

Service

    NetJets (private jets)

    FlightSafety (aircraft training)

    Business Wire (news and media)

    Pampered Chef (kitchen tools)

    Dairy Queen

    Buffalo News

    Omaha World-Herald

Retail

    Nebraska Furniture Mart

    RC Willey (home furnishings)

    Star Furniture

    Jordan's Furniture

    Borsheims (jewelry)

    Helzberg (jewelry)

    Ben Bridge (jewelry)

    See's Candies

Finance and Financial Products

    Clayton Homes (manufactured housing and finance)

    XTRA (transportation leasing)

    CORT (furniture leasing)

Source: Berkshire Hathaway 2011 annual report

REFERENCES

Introduction

John Dunn, "Georgia Tech Students Quiz Warren
  Buffett," *Georgia Tech Alumni Magazine*, Winter
  2003. http://www.nxtbook.com/nxtbooks/gatech
  /alumni-winter03/index.php?startid=17

Chapter 1: Investing

Researching Investments

"How Omaha Beats Wall Street," *Forbes*, November 1,
  1969.

Limiting Your Investments

"Three Lectures by Warren Buffett to Notre Dame
  Faculty, MBA Students and Undergraduate Students,"
  spring 1991. http://www.tilsonfunds.com
  /BuffettNotreDame.pdf

Investment and Sports

"*I call investing...*," "The Money Men," *Forbes*,
  November 1, 1974.

"*Ted Williams described...*," Lara Logan and Charlie
  Rose, "Person to Person: Warren Buffett," CBS News,
  February 8, 2012. http://www.cbsnews.com/video
  /watch/?id=7398062n

"*Degree of difficulty counts...*," Becky Quick, "Buffett's
  Worst Trade," CNBC. http://video.cnbc.com/gallery
  /?video=1618466375&play=1

Thinking about Investment

"Warren Buffett MBA Talk: Warren Buffett Talk at University of Florida," Google Video, 1:27:35, from a speech recorded on October 15, 1998. http://video .google.com/videoplay?docid=-6231308980849895261

The Temperament of an Investor

Anthony Bianco, "The Warren Buffett You Don't Know," *BusinessWeek*, July 5, 1999. http://www.businessweek .com/1999/99_27/b3636001.htm

Studying Financial Data

Letter to Berkshire Hathaway Inc. shareholders, February 27, 2009. http://www.berkshirehathaway .com/letters/letters.html

Ordinary Competence, Extraordinary Results

Carol J. Loomis, "The Inside Story of Warren Buffett," *Fortune*, April 11, 1988. http://money.cnn.com /magazines/fortune/fortune_archive/1988/04/11/70414 /index.htm

The Simplicity of Investment

"*Draw a circle…* ," "The Money Men," *Forbes*, November 1, 1974.

"*I don't know …* ," "Three Lectures by Warren Buffett to Notre Dame Faculty, MBA Students and Undergraduate Students," spring 1991. http://www .tilsonfunds.com/BuffettNotreDame.pdf

"*I have this…* ," Alice Schroeder, *The Snowball: Warren Buffett and the Business of Life* (New York: Random House, 2008).

Beating the Market

"There is no hunch…," "A Colloquium with University of
Nebraska–Lincoln Students," October 10, 1994.

"How do you beat…," Anthony Bianco, "The Warren
Buffett You Don't Know," *BusinessWeek*, July 5, 1999.
http://www.businessweek.com/1999/99_27/b3636001
.htm

"Most people can't do…," Guy Rolnick, "Warren Buffett:
The U.S. Is Moving toward Plutocracy," *Haaretz*,
March 23, 2011. http://www.haaretz.com/misc/article
-print-page/warren-buffett-the-u-s-is-moving
-toward-plutocracy-1.351236

The Advantage of Having Less Money

Anthony Bianco, "The Warren Buffett You Don't Know,"
BusinessWeek, July 5, 1999. http://www.businessweek
.com/1999/99_27/b3636001.htm

Idea Quota

"My idea quota…," "How Omaha Beats Wall Street,"
Forbes, November 1, 1969.

"When I got started…," "The Money Men," *Forbes*,
November 1, 1974.

Long-Term Investment

"I believe in owning…," "CNBC's Squawk Box: Interview
with Warren Buffett," CNBC, November 14, 2011.
http://www.cnbc.com/id/45346040

"The future is never…," "You Pay a Very High Price in
the Stock Market for a Cheery Consensus," *Forbes*,
August 6, 1979. http://www.forbes.com/2008/11/08
/buffett-forbes-article-markets-cx_pm-1107stocks
.html

"We don't want . . . ," "A Colloquium with University of
Nebraska–Lincoln Students," October 10, 1994.

Speculation vs. Investment

"CNBC's Squawk Box: Interview with Warren Buffett,"
CNBC, March 2, 2011. http://www.cnbc.com
/id/41889991

Reacting to Uncertainty

"CNBC's Squawk Box: Interview with Warren Buffett,"
CNBC, November 14, 2011. http://www.cnbc.com
/id/45346040

Diversification

"If your goal . . . ," "Warren Buffett MBA Talk: Warren
Buffett Talk at University of Florida," Google Video,
1:27:35, from a speech recorded on October 15, 1998.
http://video.google.com/videoplay
?docid=-6231308980849895261

"If you really know . . . ," "Warren Buffett MBA Talk:
Warren Buffett Talk at University of Florida," Google
Video, 1:27:35, from a speech recorded on October 15,
1998. http://video.google.com/videoplay
?docid=-6231308980849895261

Active Trading

"Anything that causes people . . . ," "CNBC's Squawk Box:
Interview with Warren Buffett," CNBC, November 14,
2011. http://www.cnbc.com/id/45346040

"Wall Street makes its money . . . ," "Warren Buffett MBA
Talk: Warren Buffett Talk at University of Florida,"
Google Video, 1:27:35, from a speech recorded on
October 15, 1998. http://video.google.com/videoplay
?docid=-6231308980849895261

"If you own a farm…," "CNBC's Squawk Box: Interview with Warren Buffett," CNBC, November 14, 2011. http://www.cnbc.com/id/45346040

"As a class…," letter to Berkshire Hathaway Inc. shareholders, February 2008. http://www.berkshirehathaway.com/letters/letters.html

Investing and the Laws of Motion

Letter to Berkshire Hathaway Inc. shareholders, February 28, 2006. http://www.berkshirehathaway.com/letters/letters.html

Buffett's First Stock

John Dunn, "Georgia Tech Students Quiz Warren Buffett," *Georgia Tech Alumni Magazine*, Winter 2003. http://www.nxtbook.com/nxtbooks/gatech/alumni-winter03/index.php?startid=17

Greed, Fear, and Buying

Warren Buffett, "Buy American. I Am," *New York Times*, October 16, 2008. http://www.nytimes.com/2008/10/17/opinion/17buffett.html

When to Buy

"I try to buy…," "How Omaha Beats Wall Street," *Forbes*, November 1, 1969.

"Imagine if you…," "How Omaha Beats Wall Street," *Forbes*, November 1, 1969.

Buying Today

"Warren Buffett and Bill Gates: Keeping America Great," transcript of a town hall meeting hosted by CNBC at Columbia University, November 12, 2009. http://www.cnbc.com/id/33901003

Silly Market Behavior

Benjamin Graham, *The Intelligent Investor: The Definitive Book on Value Investing*, Preface and Appendix by Warren Buffett (New York: HarperCollins, 2003).

Buying Troubled Companies

Anthony Bianco, "The Warren Buffett You Don't Know," *BusinessWeek*, July 5, 1999. http://www.businessweek .com/1999/99_27/b3636001.htm

Buying in the Bad Times

"Three Lectures by Warren Buffett to Notre Dame Faculty, MBA Students and Undergraduate Students," spring 1991. http://www.tilsonfunds.com /BuffettNotreDame.pdf

Pricing Stocks

"If you think . . . ," John Dunn, "Georgia Tech Students Quiz Warren Buffett," *Georgia Tech Alumni Magazine*, Winter 2003. http://www.nxtbook .com/nxtbooks/gatech/alumni-winter03/index .php?startid=17

"Whether we're talking . . . ," letter to Berkshire Hathaway Inc. shareholders, February 27, 2009. http://www .berkshirehathaway.com/letters/letters.html

The Most Important Question

"Warren Buffett MBA Talk: Warren Buffett Talk at University of Florida," Google Video, 1:27:35, from a speech recorded on October 15, 1998. http://video .google.com/videoplay?docid=-6231308980849895261

A Bird in the Hand

Alice Schroeder, *The Snowball: Warren Buffett and the Business of Life* (New York: Random House, 2008).

When Not to Buy

"Three Lectures by Warren Buffett to Notre Dame Faculty, MBA Students and Undergraduate Students," spring 1991. http://www.tilsonfunds.com /BuffettNotreDame.pdf

Buffett's Gas Station

"Warren Buffett MBA Talk: Warren Buffett Talk at University of Florida," Google Video, 1:27:35, from a speech recorded on October 15, 1998. http://video .google.com/videoplay?docid=-6231308980849895261

When to Jump Ship

Warren Buffett, *The Essays of Warren Buffett: Lessons for Corporate America*, selected, arranged, and introduced by Lawrence A. Cunningham (Durham, NC: Carolina Academic Press, 1997).

Buffett's Birth and the Market

Charlie Rose, "Warren Buffett, Investor, Philanthropist," *Charlie Rose*, September 30, 2011. http://www .charlierose.com/view/interview/11919

Hyperventilating at the Dow

Letter to Berkshire Hathaway Inc. shareholders, February 2008. http://www.berkshirehathaway.com /letters/letters.html

The Market as a Voting Machine

"The Money Men," *Forbes*, November 1, 1974.

Splitting Stocks

John Dunn, "Georgia Tech Students Quiz Warren Buffett," *Georgia Tech Alumni Magazine*, Winter 2003. http://www.nxtbook.com/nxtbooks/gatech /alumni-winter03/index.php?startid=17

Uncertainty

"CNBC's Squawk Box: Interview with Warren Buffett," CNBC, November 14, 2011. http://www.cnbc.com /id/45346040

Bonds

"CNBC's Squawk Box: Interview with Warren Buffett," CNBC, March 2, 2011. http://www.cnbc.com /id/41889991

Commodities

"CNBC's Squawk Box: Interview with Warren Buffett," CNBC, March 2, 2011. http://www.cnbc.com /id/41889991

Gold

Gold is a way . . . ," "CNBC's Squawk Box: Interview with Warren Buffett," CNBC, March 2, 2011. http://www .cnbc.com/id/41889991

You could take . . . ," Ben Stein, "Warren Buffett: Forget gold, buy stocks," *CNN, October 19, 2010.* http:// money.cnn.com/2010/10/18/pf/investing/buffett_ben _stein.fortune/index.htm

The Value of Cash

"CNBC's Squawk Box: Interview with Warren Buffett," CNBC, May 2, 2011. http://www.cnbc.com /id/42859828

Clinging to Cash

Warren Buffett, "Buy American. I Am," *New York Times*,
October 16, 2008. http://www.nytimes
.com/2008/10/17/opinion/17buffett.html

Chapter 2: Wall Street and Speculation

The Value of Wall Street

Remarks to the Financial Crisis Inquiry Commission,
May 26, 2010. http://www.scribd.com/doc/50676366
/Transcript-of-Warren-Buffett-Interview-With-FCIC

Investors in Wonderland

Letter to Berkshire Hathaway Inc. shareholders,
February 2008. http://www.berkshirehathaway.com
/letters/letters.html

Staying Sober in the Marketplace

"The Money Men," *Forbes*, November 1, 1974.

Bad Ideas on Wall Street

"Three Lectures by Warren Buffett to Notre Dame
Faculty, MBA Students and Undergraduate Students,"
spring 1991. http://www.tilsonfunds.com
/BuffettNotreDame.pdf.

Bad Terminology

Letter to Berkshire Hathaway Inc. shareholders,
February 28, 2002. http://www.berkshirehathaway
.com/letters/letters.html

The Lure of Speculation

"CNBC's Squawk Box: Interview with Warren Buffett,"
CNBC, May 2, 2011. http://www.cnbc.com
/id/42859828

Profiting from Bubbles

"CNBC's Squawk Box: Interview with Warren Buffett," CNBC, May 2, 2011. http://www.cnbc.com/id/42859828

Peer Pressure and the Cause of Bubbles

Remarks to the Financial Crisis Inquiry Commission, May 26, 2010. http://www.scribd.com/doc/50676366/Transcript-of-Warren-Buffett-Interview-With-FCIC

One More Bubble

Letter to Berkshire Hathaway Inc. shareholders, February 2008. http://www.berkshirehathaway.com/letters/letters.html

When Bubbles Burst

Guy Rolnick, "Warren Buffett: The U.S. Is Moving toward Plutocracy," *Haaretz*, March 23, 2011. http://www.haaretz.com/misc/article-print-page/warren-buffett-the-u-s-is-moving-toward-plutocracy-1.351236

Easy Money

Remarks to the Financial Crisis Inquiry Commission, May 26, 2010. http://www.scribd.com/doc/50676366/Transcript-of-Warren-Buffett-Interview-With-FCIC

Excessive Leverage

Guy Rolnick, "Warren Buffett: The U.S. Is Moving toward Plutocracy," *Haaretz*, March 23, 2011. http://www.haaretz.com/misc/article-print-page/warren-buffett-the-u-s-is-moving-toward-plutocracy-1.351236

Addictive Leverage

Letter to Berkshire Hathaway Inc. shareholders, February 26, 2011. http://www.berkshirehathaway.com/letters/letters.html

The Danger of Leverage

"Three Lectures by Warren Buffett to Notre Dame Faculty, MBA Students and Undergraduate Students," spring 1991. http://www.tilsonfunds.com/BuffettNotreDame.pdf

Smart People and Leverage

Remarks to the Financial Crisis Inquiry Commission, May 26, 2010. http://www.scribd.com/doc/50676366/Transcript-of-Warren-Buffett-Interview-With-FCIC

Derivatives

Letter to Berkshire Hathaway Inc. shareholders, February 28, 2006. http://www.berkshirehathaway.com/letters/letters.html

Credit Default Swaps

"CNBC's Squawk Box: Interview with Warren Buffett," CNBC, November 14, 2011. http://www.cnbc.com/id/45346040

Chapter 3: Businesses

Knowing Your Limits

Letter to Berkshire Hathaway Inc. shareholders, March 1, 2000. http://www.berkshirehathaway.com/letters/letters.html

Pricing Power

Remarks to the Financial Crisis Inquiry Commission,
     May 26, 2010. http://www.scribd.com/doc/50676366
     /Transcript-of-Warren-Buffett-Interview-With-FCIC

Business Moats

Letter to Berkshire Hathaway Inc. shareholders,
     February 2008. http://www.berkshirehathaway.com
     /letters/letters.html

Understanding a Business

"*We don't do . . . ,*" Anthony Bianco, "The Warren Buffett
     You Don't Know," *BusinessWeek*, July 5, 1999. http://
     www.businessweek.com/1999/99_27/b3636001.htm
"*My job is . . . ,*" "Three Lectures by Warren Buffett
     to Notre Dame Faculty, MBA Students and
     Undergraduate Students," spring 1991. http://www
     .tilsonfunds.com/BuffettNotreDame.pdf

Premium Businesses

"*One of the interesting . . . ,*" "Three Lectures by Warren
     Buffett to Notre Dame Faculty, MBA Students and
     Undergraduate Students," spring 1991. http://www
     .tilsonfunds.com/BuffettNotreDame.pdf
"*The name . . . ,*" "How Omaha Beats Wall Street," *Forbes*,
     November 1, 1969.

Capital-Intensive Businesses

"Three Lectures by Warren Buffett to Notre Dame
     Faculty, MBA Students and Undergraduate Students,"
     spring 1991. http://www.tilsonfunds.com
     /BuffettNotreDame.pdf

Finding Great Deals

"Warren Buffett and Bill Gates: Keeping America Great,"
transcript of a town hall meeting hosted by CNBC
at Columbia University, November 12, 2009. http://
www.cnbc.com/id/33901003

Newspapers

Jonathan Laing, "The Collector," *Wall Street Journal*,
March 31, 1977.

The Scuttlebutt Approach

"Warren Buffett MBA Talk: Warren Buffett Talk at
University of Florida," Google Video, 1:27:35, from a
speech recorded on October 15, 1998. http://video
.google.com/videoplay?docid=-6231308980849895261

Don't Talk to Brokers

"Three Lectures by Warren Buffett to Notre Dame
Faculty, MBA Students and Undergraduate Students,"
spring 1991. http://www.tilsonfunds.com
/BuffettNotreDame.pdf.

Knowing What You Know

Guy Rolnick, "Warren Buffett: The U.S. Is Moving
toward Plutocracy," *Haaretz*, March 23, 2011. http://
www.haaretz.com/misc/article-print-page/warren
-buffett-the-u-s-is-moving-toward-
plutocracy-1.351236

Growth vs. Profits

Letter to Berkshire Hathaway Inc. shareholders,
February 26, 2010. http://www.berkshirehathaway
.com/letters/letters.html

Buying Companies vs. Stocks

Letter to Berkshire Hathaway Inc. shareholders,
February 2008. http://www.berkshirehathaway.com
/letters/letters.html

Looking for "Elephants"

Anthony Bianco, "The Warren Buffett You Don't Know,"
BusinessWeek, July 5, 1999. http://www.businessweek
.com/1999/99_27/b3636001.htm

See's Candy

"Warren Buffett MBA Talk: Warren Buffett Talk at
University of Florida," Google Video, 1:27:35, from a
speech recorded on October 15, 1998. http://video
.google.com/videoplay?docid=-6231308980849895261

Coca-Cola and Happiness

"Warren Buffett MBA Talk: Warren Buffett Talk at
University of Florida," Google Video, 1:27:35, from a
speech recorded on October 15, 1998. http://video
.google.com/videoplay?docid=-6231308980849895261

The Taste of Colas

"Warren Buffett MBA Talk: Warren Buffett Talk at
University of Florida," Google Video, 1:27:35, from a
speech recorded on October 15, 1998. http://video
.google.com/videoplay?docid=-6231308980849895261

Hershey's

"Three Lectures by Warren Buffett to Notre Dame
Faculty, MBA Students and Undergraduate Students,"
http://www.tilsonfunds.com/BuffettNotreDame.pdf

Gillette

"A Colloquium with University of Nebraska–Lincoln Students," October 10, 1994.

The *Daily Racing Form*

"Three Lectures by Warren Buffett to Notre Dame Faculty, MBA Students and Undergraduate Students," http://www.tilsonfunds.com/BuffettNotreDame.pdf.

The Walt Disney Company

"*Look at what...*," "How Omaha Beats Wall Street," *Forbes*, November 1, 1969.

"*We bought 5 percent...*," "Three Lectures by Warren Buffett to Notre Dame Faculty, MBA Students and Undergraduate Students," spring 1991. http://www.tilsonfunds.com/BuffettNotreDame.pdf

Making Money from the Internet

Anthony Bianco, "The Warren Buffett You Don't Know," *BusinessWeek*, July 5, 1999. http://www.businessweek.com/1999/99_27/b3636001.htm

The Hype of Internet Companies

Remarks to the Financial Crisis Inquiry Commission, May 26, 2010. http://www.scribd.com/doc/50676366/Transcript-of-Warren-Buffett-Interview-With-FCIC

Textiles

"*Our textile business...*," "Three Lectures by Warren Buffett to Notre Dame Faculty, MBA Students and Undergraduate Students," spring 1991. http://www.tilsonfunds.com/BuffettNotreDame.pdf

Corporate Ethics

Letter to Berkshire Hathaway Inc. shareholders,
February 21, 2003. http://www.berkshirehathaway
.com/letters/letters.html

Exposed Companies

Letter to Berkshire Hathaway Inc. shareholders,
February 2008. http://www.berkshirehathaway.com
/letters/letters.html

Risk and Human Nature

"CNBC's Squawk Box: Interview with Warren Buffett,"
CNBC, November 14, 2011. http://www.cnbc.com
/id/45346040

The High Road in Corporate America

Letter to Berkshire Hathaway Inc. shareholders,
February 2008. http://www.berkshirehathaway.com
/letters/letters.html

Inflated Earnings

Warren Buffett, "Who Really Cooks the Books?," *New
York Times*, July 24, 2002. http://www.nytimes
.com/2002/07/24/opinion/who-really-cooks-the
-books.html

Dirty Corporate Laundry

John Dunn, "Georgia Tech Students Quiz Warren
Buffett," *Georgia Tech Alumni Magazine*, Winter
2003. http://www.nxtbook.com/nxtbooks/gatech
/alumni-winter03/index.php?startid=17

Accounting for Stock Options

Letter to Berkshire Hathaway Inc. shareholders, March 1, 1999. http://www.berkshirehathaway.com /letters/letters.html

CEO Ethics

Letter to Berkshire Hathaway Inc. shareholders, February 21, 2003. http://www.berkshirehathaway .com/letters/letters.html

Chapter 4: Berkshire Hathaway

One Good Decision

Lara Logan and Charlie Rose, "Person to Person: Warren Buffett," CBS News, February 8, 2012. http://www .cbsnews.com/video/watch/?id=7398062

The Importance of a Good Decision

Remarks to the Financial Crisis Inquiry Commission, May 26, 2010. http://www.scribd.com/doc/50676366 /Transcript-of-Warren-Buffett-Interview-With-FCIC

More Money than Ideas

Anthony Bianco, "The Warren Buffett You Don't Know," *BusinessWeek*, July 5, 1999. http://www.businessweek .com/1999/99_27/b3636001.htm

Making Mistakes

"Mistakes don't bother me . . . ," Guy Rolnick, "Warren Buffett: The U.S. Is Moving toward Plutocracy," *Haaretz*, March 23, 2011. http://www.haaretz.com /misc/article-print-page/warren-buffett-the-u-s-is -moving-toward-plutocracy-1.351236

"I'll make more mistakes … ," letter to Berkshire
Hathaway Inc. shareholders, February 2008. http://
www.berkshirehathaway.com/letters/letters.html

Never Looking Back

"Warren Buffett MBA Talk: Warren Buffett Talk at
University of Florida," Google Video, 1:27:35, from a
speech recorded on October 15, 1998. http://video
.google.com/videoplay?docid=-6231308980849895261

Mistakes of Omission

John Dunn, "Georgia Tech Students Quiz Warren
Buffett," *Georgia Tech Alumni Magazine*, Winter
2003. http://www.nxtbook.com/nxtbooks/gatech
/alumni-winter03/index.php?startid=17

Making Money Together

Warren Buffett, *The Essays of Warren Buffett: Lessons
for Corporate America*, selected, arranged, and
introduced by Lawrence A. Cunningham (Durham,
NC: Carolina Academic Press, 1997).

Structuring Deals

Guy Rolnick, "Warren Buffett: The U.S. Is Moving
toward Plutocracy," *Haaretz*, March 23, 2011. http://
www.haaretz.com/misc/article-print-page/warren
-buffett-the-u-s-is-moving-toward-
plutocracy-1.351236

Overseeing Berkshire's Businesses

Letter to Berkshire Hathaway Inc. shareholders,
February 26, 2010. http://www.berkshirehathaway
.com/letters/letters.html

Holding Onto Businesses

Anthony Bianco, "The Warren Buffett You Don't Know,"
BusinessWeek, July 5, 1999. http://www.businessweek
.com/1999/99_27/b3636001.htm

Selling Subpar Businesses

Warren Buffett, *The Essays of Warren Buffett: Lessons
for Corporate America*, selected, arranged, and
introduced by Lawrence A. Cunningham (Durham,
NC: Carolina Academic Press, 1997).

No Exit Strategy

Letter to Berkshire Hathaway Inc. shareholders,
February 21, 2003. http://www.berkshirehathaway
.com/letters/letters.html

Berkshire's Congregation

"Warren Buffett MBA Talk: Warren Buffett Talk at
University of Florida," Google Video, 1:27:35, from a
speech recorded on October 15, 1998. http://video
.google.com/videoplay?docid=-6231308980849895261

Paying Berkshire's Directors

Letter to Berkshire Hathaway Inc. shareholders,
February 21, 2003. http://www.berkshirehathaway
.com/letters/letters.html

Institutional Failure and CEO Compensation

Remarks to the Financial Crisis Inquiry Commission,
May 26, 2010. http://www.scribd.com/doc/50676366
/Transcript-of-Warren-Buffett-Interview-With-FCIC

Inflating CEOs

Remarks to the Financial Crisis Inquiry Commission,
May 26, 2010. http://www.scribd.com/doc/50676366
/Transcript-of-Warren-Buffett-Interview-With-FCIC

The Qualities of a Good Director

Letter to Berkshire Hathaway Inc. shareholders,
February 21, 2003. http://www.berkshirehathaway
.com/letters/letters.html

How Not to Choose Directors

Letter to Berkshire Hathaway Inc. shareholders,
February 28, 2007. http://www.berkshirehathaway
.com/letters/letters.html

Overpaying CEOs

Letter to Berkshire Hathaway Inc. shareholders,
February 28, 2006. http://www.berkshirehathaway
.com/letters/letters.html

Paying for CEO Performance

Remarks to the Financial Crisis Inquiry Commission,
May 26, 2010. http://www.scribd.com/doc/50676366
/Transcript-of-Warren-Buffett-Interview-With-FCIC

Replacing CEOs

Letter to Berkshire Hathaway Inc. shareholders,
February 21, 2003. http://www.berkshirehathaway
.com/letters/letters.html

CEOs and Negative Reinforcement

"Warren Buffett and Bill Gates: Keeping America Great,"
transcript of a town hall meeting hosted by CNBC
at Columbia University, November 12, 2009. http://
www.cnbc.com/id/33901003

CEO Perks

"*You've read . . . ,*" letter to Berkshire Hathaway Inc. shareholders, February 28, 2007. http://www .berkshirehathaway.com/letters/letters.html

"*Huge severance payments . . . ,*" letter to Berkshire Hathaway Inc. shareholders, February 28, 2006. http://www.berkshirehathaway.com/letters/letters .html

Managers Thinking Like Owners

"*I like guys who . . . ,*" Jonathan Laing, "The Collector," *Wall Street Journal*, March 31, 1977.

"*We have a business . . . ,*" "Three Lectures by Warren Buffett to Notre Dame Faculty, MBA Students and Undergraduate Students," spring 1991. http://www .tilsonfunds.com/BuffettNotreDame.pdf

Berkshire's Managers

Letter to Berkshire Hathaway Inc. shareholders, February 21, 2003. http://www.berkshirehathaway .com/letters/letters.html

Managing Winners

Letter to Berkshire Hathaway Inc. shareholders, February 21, 2003. http://www.berkshirehathaway .com/letters/letters.html

Using Smart People

Shereen Bhan, "Warren Buffett: I Don't Have to Be Smart about Everything," *Forbes India*, April 20, 2011. http://forbesindia.com/printcontent/24142?id=24142

Cost-Consciousness

Letter to Berkshire Hathaway Inc. shareholders,
February 21, 2003. http://www.berkshirehathaway
.com/letters/letters.html

Cutting Costs

Carol J. Loomis, "The Inside Story of Warren Buffett,"
Fortune, April 11, 1988. http://money.cnn.com
/magazines/fortune/fortune_
archive/1988/04/11/70414/index.htm

Managing Workers

Warren Buffett, *The Essays of Warren Buffett: Lessons
for Corporate America*, selected, arranged, and
introduced by Lawrence A. Cunningham (Durham,
NC: Carolina Academic Press, 1997).

Letting Managers Manage

"Usually the managers…," Warren Buffett, *The Essays of
Warren Buffett: Lessons for Corporate America*, selected,
arranged, and introduced by Lawrence A. Cunningham
(Durham, NC: Carolina Academic Press, 1997).

"There are many…," Letter to Berkshire Hathaway Inc.
shareholders, February 28, 2007. http://www
.berkshirehathaway.com/letters/letters.html

The Reputations of Managers

Becky Quick, "Buffett's Worst Trade," CNBC. http://
video.cnbc.com/gallery/?video=1618466375&play=1

Jay-Z, Business Man

Evelyn M. Rusli, "Buffett Returns to Cartoonland,
Joined by Jay-Z," *New York Times*, October 18, 2011.
http://dealbook.nytimes.com/2011/10/18/buffett
-returns-to-cartoonland-joined-by-jay-z/

Hiring

"*We don't hire…*," Ben Stein, "Warren Buffett: Forget Gold, Buy Stocks," *CNN, October 19, 2010.* http://money.cnn.com/2010/10/18/pf/investing/buffett_ben_stein.fortune/index.htm

Enjoying Work

"A Colloquium with University of Nebraska–Lincoln Students," October 10, 1994.

Chapter 5: US Policies and Politics

Betting on the United States

"CNBC's Squawk Box: Interview with Warren Buffett," CNBC, May 2, 2011. http://www.cnbc.com/id/42859828

Economic Recovery

"*I think the big factor…*," "CNBC's Squawk Box: Interview with Warren Buffett," CNBC, May 2, 2011. http://www.cnbc.com/id/42859828

"*GEICO got in trouble…*," Charlie Rose, "Warren Buffett, Investor, Philanthropist," *Charlie Rose*, September 30, 2011. http://www.charlierose.com/view/interview/11919

The United States since 1930

"*I was born in August of 1930 …*," "CNBC's Squawk Box: Interview with Warren Buffett," CNBC, July 7, 2011. http://www.cnbc.com/id/43671706

"*I'm 80 years old…*," Guy Rolnick, "Warren Buffett: The U.S. Is Moving toward Plutocracy," *Haaretz*, March 23, 2011. http://www.haaretz.com/misc/article-print-page/warren-buffett-the-u-s-is-moving-toward-plutocracy-1.351236

The United States Solves Problems

"Warren Buffett and Bill Gates: Keeping America Great," transcript of a town hall meeting hosted by CNBC at Columbia University, November 12, 2009. http://www.cnbc.com/id/33901003

Economic Forecasts

"I don't read economic forecasts.... ," Anthony Bianco, "The Warren Buffett You Don't Know," *BusinessWeek*, July 5, 1999. http://www.businessweek.com/1999/99_27/b3636001.htm

"We have never bought... ," "Warren Buffett MBA Talk: Warren Buffett Talk at University of Florida," Google Video, 1:27:35, from a speech recorded on October 15, 1998. http://video.google.com/videoplay?docid=-6231308980849895261

Global Trade

Shereen Bhan, "Warren Buffett: I Don't Have to Be Smart about Everything," *Forbes India*, April 20, 2011. http://forbesindia.com/printcontent/24142?id=24142

Creating Jobs

"CNBC's Squawk Box: Interview with Warren Buffett," CNBC, November 14, 2011. http://www.cnbc.com/id/45346040

Inflation

"Inflation, someone... ," Shereen Bhan, "Warren Buffett: I Don't Have to Be Smart about Everything," *Forbes India*, April 20, 2011. http://forbesindia.com/printcontent/24142?id=24142

"Every time I get worried… ," Guy Rolnick, "Warren
  Buffett: The U.S. Is Moving toward Plutocracy,"
  Haaretz, March 23, 2011. http://www.haaretz.com
  /misc/article-print-page/warren-buffett-the-u-s-is
  -moving-toward-plutocracy-1.351236

The 2008 Financial Crisis

"People were… ," Remarks to the Financial Crisis Inquiry
  Commission, May 26, 2010. http://www.scribd
  .com/doc/50676366/Transcript-of-Warren-Buffett
  -Interview-With-FCIC

"The American people… ," Guy Rolnick, "Warren Buffett:
  The U.S. Is Moving toward Plutocracy," *Haaretz*,
  March 23, 2011. http://www.haaretz.com/misc/article
  -print-page/warren-buffett-the-u-s-is-moving
  -toward-plutocracy-1.351236

"When it really… ," Remarks to the Financial Crisis
  Inquiry Commission, May 26, 2010. http://www
  .scribd.com/doc/50676366/Transcript-of-Warren
  -Buffett-Interview-With-FCIC

Government Intervention in the Financial Crisis

"Whatever the downsides… ," Remarks to the Financial
  Crisis Inquiry Commission, May 26, 2010. http://
  www.scribd.com/doc/50676366/Transcript-of
  -Warren-Buffett-Interview-With-FCIC

"Only the government… ," "Warren Buffett and Bill
  Gates: Keeping America Great," transcript of a town
  hall meeting hosted by CNBC at Columbia University,
  November 12, 2009. http://www.cnbc
  .com/id/33901003

"We should thank Bernanke… ," "CNBC's Squawk Box:
  Interview with Warren Buffett," CNBC, November 14,
  2011. http://www.cnbc.com/id/45346040

Bank of America and the Financial Crisis

Remarks to the Financial Crisis Inquiry Commission,
May 26, 2010. http://www.scribd.com/doc/50676366
/Transcript-of-Warren-Buffett-Interview-With-FCIC

Opportunities during the Financial Crisis

"Warren Buffett and Bill Gates: Keeping America Great,"
transcript of a town hall meeting hosted by CNBC
at Columbia University, November 12, 2009. http://
www.cnbc.com/id/33901003

The Importance of Credit

Letter to Berkshire Hathaway Inc. shareholders,
February 26, 2011. http://www.berkshirehathaway
.com/letters/letters.html

Fraud in the Financial System

Remarks to the Financial Crisis Inquiry Commission,
May 26, 2010. http://www.scribd.com/doc/50676366
/Transcript-of-Warren-Buffett-Interview-With-FCIC

Lending after the Financial Crisis

"Charlie Rose, "Warren Buffett, Investor,
Philanthropist," *Charlie Rose*, September 30, 2011.
http://www.charlierose.com/view/interview/11919

The US Budget and Trade Deficits

"CNBC's Squawk Box: Interview with Warren Buffett,"
CNBC, November 14, 2011. http://www.cnbc.com
/id/45346040

The Simpson-Bowles Plan

"CNBC's Squawk Box: Interview with Warren Buffett,"
CNBC, November 14, 2011. http://www.cnbc.com
/id/45346040

Government Debt

"Three Lectures by Warren Buffett to Notre Dame Faculty, MBA Students and Undergraduate Students," spring 1991. http://www.tilsonfunds.com /BuffettNotreDame.pdf

Raising the Debt Ceiling

"CNBC's Squawk Box: Interview with Warren Buffett," CNBC, July 7, 2011. http://www.cnbc.com/id/43671706

Democracy in the United States

Guy Rolnick, "Warren Buffett: The U.S. Is Moving toward Plutocracy," *Haaretz*, March 23, 2011. http:// www.haaretz.com/misc/article-print-page/warren -buffett-the-u-s-is-moving-toward- plutocracy-1.351236

The Death of Osama Bin Laden

"CNBC's Squawk Box: Interview with Warren Buffett," CNBC, May 2, 2011. http://www.cnbc.com /id/42859828

September 11, 2001

"*I really thought…*," "CNBC's Squawk Box: Interview with Warren Buffett," CNBC, May 2, 2011. http:// www.cnbc.com/id/42859828

"*Why, you might ask…*," letter to Berkshire Hathaway Inc. shareholders, February 28, 2002. http://www .berkshirehathaway.com/letters/letters.html

China

"CNBC's Squawk Box: Interview with Warren Buffett," CNBC, November 14, 2011. http://www.cnbc.com /id/45346040

The Euro Crisis

Charlie Rose, "Warren Buffett, Investor, Philanthropist,"
Charlie Rose, September 30, 2011. http://www
.charlierose.com/view/interview/11919

Barack Obama

Charlie Rose, "Warren Buffett, Investor, Philanthropist,"
Charlie Rose, September 30, 2011. http://www
.charlierose.com/view/interview/11919

Chapter 6: Wealth and Taxes

Possessions

Lara Logan and Charlie Rose, "Person to Person: Warren
Buffett," CBS News, February 8, 2012. http://www
.cbsnews.com/video/watch/?id=7398062n

Money's Magnifying Power

John Dunn, "Georgia Tech Students Quiz Warren
Buffett," *Georgia Tech Alumni Magazine*, Winter
2003. http://www.nxtbook.com/nxtbooks/gatech
/alumni-winter03/index.php?startid=17

Wealth and Satisfaction

"CNBC's Squawk Box: Interview with Warren Buffett,"
CNBC, November 14, 2011. http://www.cnbc.com
/id/45346040

Dividing the Economic Pie

Guy Rolnick, "Warren Buffett: The U.S. Is Moving
toward Plutocracy," *Haaretz*, March 23, 2011. http://
www.haaretz.com/misc/article-print-page/warren
-buffett-the-u-s-is-moving-toward-
plutocracy-1.351236

The Rising Tide of Wealth

Lara Logan and Charlie Rose, "Person to Person: Warren Buffett," CBS News, February 8, 2012. http://www .cbsnews.com/video/watch/?id=7398062n

The Source of Buffett's Wealth

"My wealth has ... ," Warren Buffett, The Giving Pledge. http://givingpledge.org/#warren_buffett

"When we got married ... ," Carol J. Loomis, "A Conversation with Warren Buffett," *Fortune*, June 25, 2006. http://money.cnn.com/2006/06/25/magazines /fortune/charity2.fortune/

Inheritance

"A very rich person ... ," Carol J. Loomis, "A Conversation with Warren Buffett," *Fortune*, June 25, 2006. http:// money.cnn.com/2006/06/25/magazines/fortune /charity2.fortune/

"Neither Susie nor I ... ," Carol J. Loomis, "A Conversation with Warren Buffett," *Fortune*, June 25, 2006. http://money.cnn.com/2006/06/25/magazines /fortune/charity2.fortune/

"Wealth is just a bunch ... ," Alice Schroeder, *The Snowball: Warren Buffett and the Business of Life* (New York: Random House, 2008).

Buffett's Good Fortune

"If all of us were stranded ... ," "Warren Buffett MBA Talk: Warren Buffett Talk at University of Florida," Google Video, 1:27:35, from a speech recorded on October 15, 1998. http://video.google.com/videoplay ?docid=-6231308980849895261

"I was born at the right time…," Anthony Bianco, "The Warren Buffett You Don't Know," *BusinessWeek*, July 5, 1999. http://www.businessweek.com/1999/99_27/b3636001.htm

"I have been lucky…," "Warren Buffett MBA Talk: Warren Buffett Talk at University of Florida," Google Video, 1:27:35, from a speech recorded on October 15, 1998. http://video.google.com/videoplay?docid=-6231308980849895261

Wealthy People's Tax Rates

"I'll bet a million dollars…," Tom Brokaw, "Interview with Warren Buffett," *NBC Nightly News*, October 30, 2007. http://www.cnbc.com/id/21553857

"Forty percent of the revenue…," "CNBC's Squawk Box: Interview with Warren Buffett," CNBC, July 7, 2011. http://www.cnbc.com/id/43671706

Taxes for Hedge Fund Operators

Tom Brokaw, "Interview with Warren Buffett," *NBC Nightly News*, October 30, 2007. http://www.cnbc.com/id/21553857

Shared Sacrifice

Warren Buffett, "Stop Coddling the Super-Rich," *New York Times*, August 14, 2011. http://www.nytimes.com/2011/08/15/opinion/stop-coddling-the-super-rich.html

The Estate Tax

Alice Schroeder, *The Snowball: Warren Buffett and the Business of Life* (New York: Random House, 2008).

Berkshire's Tax Bill

Letter to Berkshire Hathaway Inc. shareholders, March 1, 1999. http://www.berkshirehathaway.com/letters/letters.html

Revenue-Neutral Tax Reform

"CNBC's Squawk Box: Interview with Warren Buffett," CNBC, November 14, 2011. http://www.cnbc.com/id/45346040

Lobbying and the Tax Code

Every line in the tax code . . . ," Guy Rolnick, "Warren Buffett: The U.S. Is Moving toward Plutocracy," *Haaretz*, March 23, 2011. http://www.haaretz.com/misc/article-print-page/warren-buffett-the-u-s-is-moving-toward-plutocracy-1.351236

"*The tax law has been shaped . . . ,*" "CNBC's Squawk Box: Interview with Warren Buffett," CNBC, July 7, 2011. http://www.cnbc.com/id/43671706

Income Inequality

"*If you look at these . . . ,*" Charlie Rose, "Warren Buffett, Investor, Philanthropist," *Charlie Rose*, September 30, 2011. http://www.charlierose.com/view/interview/11919

"*If there's a class war . . . ,*" "CNBC's Squawk Box: Interview with Warren Buffett," CNBC, November 14, 2011. http://www.cnbc.com/id/45346040

"*This system works . . . ,*" "CNBC's Squawk Box: Interview with Warren Buffett," CNBC, November 14, 2011.

The "Buffett Rule"

"In the last…," "CNBC's Squawk Box: Interview with Warren Buffett," CNBC, November 14, 2011. http://www.cnbc.com/id/45346040

"It's very important…," Charlie Rose, "Warren Buffett, Investor, Philanthropist," *Charlie Rose*, September 30, 2011. http://www.charlierose.com/view/interview/11919

"I'd rather have…," "CNBC's Squawk Box: Interview with Warren Buffett," CNBC, November 14, 2011. http://www.cnbc.com/id/45346040

Chapter 7: Life Lessons

Unconditional Love

Willow Bay, "Warren Buffett Interview: The Best Life Advice I've Ever Received," *Huffington Post*, July 8, 2010. http://www.huffingtonpost.com/2010/07/08/warren-buffett-interview_n_639536.html

Buffett's Father

"My dad … he was really …," Alice Schroeder, *The Snowball: Warren Buffett and the Business of Life* (New York: Random House, 2008).

"I never saw my dad …," Lara Logan and Charlie Rose, "Person to Person: Warren Buffett," CBS News, February 8, 2012. http://www.cbsnews.com/video/watch/?id=7398062n

Buffett's Advantages

Alice Schroeder, *The Snowball: Warren Buffett and the Business of Life* (New York: Random House, 2008).

Childhood Rebellion

Alice Schroeder, *The Snowball: Warren Buffett and the Business of Life* (New York: Random House, 2008).

Learning Ethics

"Warren Buffett and Bill Gates: Keeping America Great," transcript of a town hall meeting hosted by CNBC at Columbia University, November 12, 2009. http://www.cnbc.com/id/33901003

Buffett's Wife

Alice Schroeder, *The Snowball: Warren Buffett and the Business of Life* (New York: Random House, 2008).

Whom to Marry

"Warren Buffett and Bill Gates: Keeping America Great," transcript of a town hall meeting hosted by CNBC at Columbia University, November 12, 2009. http://www.cnbc.com/id/33901003

Life Plans

"How Omaha Beats Wall Street," *Forbes*, November 1, 1969.

Teasing Jay-Z

Lara Logan and Charlie Rose, "Person to Person: Warren Buffett," CBS News, February 8, 2012. http://www.cbsnews.com/video/watch/?id=7398062n

Daily Routine

"A Colloquium with University of Nebraska–Lincoln Students," October 10, 1994.

Patience

Willow Bay, "Warren Buffett Interview: The Best Life
Advice I've Ever Received," *Huffington Post*, July 8,
2010. http://www.huffingtonpost.com/2010/07/08
/warren-buffett-interview_n_639536.html

Belief in Oneself

"I feel like I'm ... ," Alice Schroeder, *The Snowball:
Warren Buffett and the Business of Life* (New York:
Random House, 2008).

"I do not believe ... ," "A Colloquium with University of
Nebraska–Lincoln Students," October 10, 1994.

Whom Buffett Listens To

"Warren Buffett and Bill Gates: Keeping America Great,"
transcript of a town hall meeting hosted by CNBC
at Columbia University, November 12, 2009. http://
www.cnbc.com/id/33901003

The Inner Scorecard

Alice Schroeder, *The Snowball: Warren Buffett and the
Business of Life* (New York: Random House, 2008).

Your Best Investment

John Dunn, "Georgia Tech Students Quiz Warren
Buffett," *Georgia Tech Alumni Magazine*, Winter
2003. http://www.nxtbook.com/nxtbooks/gatech
/alumni-winter03/index.php?startid=17

Unpleasant Work

John Dunn, "Georgia Tech Students Quiz Warren
Buffett," *Georgia Tech Alumni Magazine*, Winter
2003. http://www.nxtbook.com/nxtbooks/gatech
/alumni-winter03/index.php?startid=17

Loving Your Work

"You gotta do…," John Dunn, "Georgia Tech Students Quiz Warren Buffett," *Georgia Tech Alumni Magazine*, Winter 2003. http://www.nxtbook. com/nxtbooks/gatech/alumni-winter03/index. php?startid=17

"Do what you would do…," "Warren Buffett and Bill Gates: Keeping America Great," transcript of a town hall meeting hosted by CNBC at Columbia University, November 12, 2009. http:// www.cnbc.com/id/33901003

Integrity

"Warren Buffett MBA Talk: Warren Buffett Talk at University of Florida," Google Video, 1:27:35, from a speech recorded on October 15, 1998. http://video .google.com/videoplay?docid=-6231308980849895261

Qualities for Success

"Warren Buffett MBA Talk: Warren Buffett talk at University of Florida," Google Video, 1:27:35, from a speech recorded on October 15, 1998. http://video .google.com/videoplay?docid=-6231308980849895261

Temperament

"Three Lectures by Warren Buffett to Notre Dame Faculty, MBA Students and Undergraduate Students," spring 1991. http://www.tilsonfunds.com /BuffettNotreDame.pdf

Old Age

Lara Logan and Charlie Rose, "Person to Person: Warren Buffett," CBS News, February 8, 2012. http://www .cbsnews.com/video/watch/?id=7398062n

Measuring Success

John Dunn, "Georgia Tech Students Quiz Warren Buffett," *Georgia Tech Alumni Magazine*, Winter 2003. http://www.nxtbook.com/nxtbooks/gatech /alumni-winter03/index.php?startid=17

Taking Care of Yourself

Alice Schroeder, *The Snowball: Warren Buffett and the Business of Life* (New York: Random House, 2008).

The Forbes List

"CNBC's Squawk Box: Interview with Warren Buffett," CNBC, May 2, 2011. http://www.cnbc.com /id/42859828

Retiring

"CNBC's Squawk Box: Interview with Warren Buffett," CNBC, November 14, 2011. http://www.cnbc.com /id/45346040

Managing Posthumously

Letter to Berkshire Hathaway Inc. shareholders, February 2008. http://www.berkshirehathaway.com /letters/letters.html

The Challenges of Philanthropy

Guy Rolnick, "Warren Buffett: The U.S. Is Moving toward Plutocracy," *Haaretz*, March 23, 2011. http:// www.haaretz.com/misc/article-print-page/warren -buffett-the-u-s-is-moving-toward- plutocracy-1.351236

Giving Back to Society

Carol J. Loomis, "A Conversation with Warren Buffett," *Fortune*, June 25, 2006. http://money.cnn.com/2006/06/25/magazines/fortune/charity2.fortune/

Giving to the Gates Foundation

"I came to realize that … ," Carol J. Loomis, "A Conversation with Warren Buffett," *Fortune*, June 25, 2006. http://money.cnn.com/2006/06/25/magazines/fortune/charity2.fortune/

"He has this view … ," "Warren Buffett and Bill Gates: Keeping America Great," transcript of a town hall meeting hosted by CNBC at Columbia University, November 12, 2009. http://www.cnbc.com/id/33901003

"I'm getting two people … ," Carol J. Loomis, "A Conversation with Warren Buffett," *Fortune*, June 25, 2006. http://money.cnn.com/2006/06/25/magazines/fortune/charity2.fortune/

A Fair Society

"Warren Buffett MBA Talk: Warren Buffett Talk at University of Florida," Google Video, 1:27:35, from a speech recorded on October 15, 1998. http://video.google.com/videoplay?docid=-6231308980849895261